Who Shall We Be?

Mary I. Farr

Copyright © 2025 by Mary I. Farr

All rights reserved. No part of this book may be used or reproduced in any manner whatsoever without written permission, except in the case of brief quotations embodied in critical articles or reviews.

Illustrations by Hannah Farr

Published 2025 by Shorehouse Books

Printed in the United States of America

ISBN-13: 979-8-9894863-9-7

DEDICATION

I dedicate this book to my dear father, Merrill Farr, a respected circuit court judge and an exceptional storyteller. From history to humor, he recognized the value of words and encouraged me to write.

Table of Contents

First Words
Who Shall We Be, A Love Letter to a Wounded World 1
Where does Hope Hide When We Need It? 5
The Power of Story 18
Belonging Nurtures Personal and Community Wellbeing 25
Not Belonging Invites Isolation and Loneliness 34
Looking for Meaning 44
Leading With Love 52
Wisdom Wellness - An idea that has come alive 64
Hooray for Homeys 76
My Wise Friend Iris 87
Healing Born of Gratitude 100
An Informed Response to Immigration 110
Are We Awake Yet? 123
Retire or transition? This is the question 134
Today I Will Choose Joy—A discussion guide 145

First Words

Who Shall We Be, A Love Letter to a Wounded World

How do we, as individuals, families, and communities, live, grow, heal, and hope in a struggling world? The list of concerns is long: racial and cultural divides, political power struggles, besieged faith traditions, and unspeakable violence.

The stories and reflections contained in the following pages invite readers to engage in honest self-examination with a commitment to hope. Who are we today? Who could we be going forward? How do we recognize and apply our gifts to enhance the quality of our families, communities and beyond? My purpose in writing this book is to enlighten, encourage, and invite readers to live more fully and creatively into their own peace building gifts."

"Don't ask what the world needs. Ask what makes you come alive and go do it. Because the world needs people who have come alive."

Mary Farr

These are the words of The Rev. Howard Thurman, an African American theologian who played a leading role in numerous social justice movements and organizations of the 20th century. He was one of the principal architects of the modern, nonviolent civil rights movement and a key mentor to Dr. Martin Luther King Jr. Reverend Thurman's work frequently includes the topic of "creative intelligence." He describes it as a quality infused in our lives and faith. In other words, each of us holds the capacity to come alive with creative intelligence.

So, what is creative intelligence? Why does it matter, and how do we recognize it? It's a term that originated in the field of psychology. It pertains to one's ability to solve problems by imagining new and unique solutions. Creative intelligence is strongly associated with individuals who have a knack for storytelling, art, and developing or repurposing ideas. Someone with creative intelligence would be highly innovative and imaginative.

Creative intelligence does not necessarily make headlines or buckets of money. When we talk about it within the context of our communities and among ourselves, we are talking about how to use our own gifts and life experience in ways that

Who Shall We Be?

foster new insight, new possibilities, or new connections. One might say, it's like repurposing an idea or product. Additionally, if we possess this gift that has the potential to manifest itself in different and constructive ways, our task, is to identify how it could support and enhance our relationships within our families, communities, and all those with whom we interact. So, how can we share these gifts in creative ways that bring us joy and make the world better. What does it feel like to "be alive?

Let me offer a small example. Recently while walking my dog, I encountered a shrieking, red-shouldered hawk tangled in bird netting. As startling as it was, I impulsively grabbed the splendid bird and held on until it calmed down. Unable to free it from its predicament, I ripped the netting off the shrub and ran with my barking and leaping dog toward an open garage hoping to find help. A woman with scissors appeared and agreed to attempt to cut the bird free. It resulted in nearly an hour of delicate snipping. The hawk, though a fierce predator in its own world, never made a sound or showed aggression toward either of us.

This experience has become a metaphor for me, an image of a larger truth about how we, as creatures of the earth, need to "cut through the nets." We need one another in our mourning our problem solving, our politics and education. We need one another in our fears, anger, and willingness to sacrifice on behalf of ourselves and others.

It doesn't matter how gifted, wealthy, or how powerful we are. We simply can't go it alone. None of these qualities keep us from getting sick or from losing our homes in wildfires or tornados. None of these qualities guarantees we won't lose our job or our life savings. We need one another. We need community not chaos.

So, where do we go from here? Who shall we be? How do we live in and through the world's tension in which we find ourselves. I believe we are being called to love beyond our homes and faith communities—not sentimental, naïve love but a practical, unpolished kind that shows up and seeks good for others as well as for ourselves.

"Who Shall We Be," is an example of my commitment to repurpose my writing in ways that encourage readers to explore our combined potential to become a beloved community.

Who Shall We Be?

Where does Hope Hide When We Need It?

Shortly after September 11 when New York City bore the blow of commercial aircraft, I heard a curious story on National Public Radio. The reporter of the story had been in Brooklyn on that fateful day and happened upon a neighborhood park shortly after the first plane hit the World Trade Center. People had congregated in the park to gaze in disbelief at the smoldering skyline. Clutched in twos and threes, they hunkered around portable radios, incredulous over the emerging details of what they were witnessing. With morning coffee still cooling in their cups and leashed dogs straining to meet their canine neighbors, each of the observers struggled to grasp the significance of the horrific event they watch unfolding from a distance.

After observing the worried gathering for some time, the reporter noticed a single individual at the far edge of the park. Unlike the others, this fellow had no coffee or family pet at his side. He did, however, have a set of golf clubs and a large basked of balls. With a seven iron in hand, he methodically placed one ball after another in front of him. Then he carefully arranged his feet and corrected his grip before driving each ball into a field of tall grass on the other side of the street.

The golfer then made no attempt to retrieve his golf balls, nor did he look up at the fiery, concrete skyline crumbling before him. The reporter watched with curiosity, trying to understand the man's apparent indifference to the mounting catastrophe. Torn between his desire to learn the answer and his reluctance to invade a stranger's privacy, the reporter finally got out of his car and approached the golfer.

"Good morning. Excuse me, but do you know what has taken place at the World Trade Center," the reporter queried cautiously. Silence. "Do you often come to this park to hit golf balls?" He persisted, though received no response from the golfer.

Who Shall We Be?

After another long silence, the golfer surprised the reporter with a reply. "Yes, I do know what has taken place." He then addressed yet another ball and drove it into the tall grass. "I know what I've heard. I don't understand it, and I can't do anything about it," he added, as he, continued to engage in his driving exercise. "But I know how to hit these golf balls."

I heard this story while driving to Albany, New York to catch a flight back to Minnesota after visiting family and friends in Vermont. Of course, there were no flights back to Minnesota that day, or for the next ten days. All this gave me time to reflect on the magnitude of the Twin Towers crisis and what it meant for ourselves and our country.

My delay in coming home meant that I would spend the next ten days meeting with friends and neighbors to discuss the state of our country. We each struggled with questions about what had become of our sense of safety and hope? I also joined a prayer group that met daily at a local church. Shortly after that, the minister of this church invited me to preach on the upcoming Sunday morning. The selected reading from Ecclesiastes that morning was one we've likely heard in the form of song lyrics and nostalgic reflections.

Ironically, the author of Ecclesiastes might be the most pessimistic and negative teacher in either the Old or New Testament. He rails on about the vanities of life and how nothing matters. He is very critical and may well have been expressing a growing skepticism within a segment of Israelite society.

In the Hebrew Bible, the book of Ecclesiastes is called Qoheleth, which means assembly or congregation—ecclesia. Qoheleth is what we call a wisdom figure, and it appears that his purpose was not so much to teach about God, but rather to tell what he had discovered about life, what humans might gain from life. He sets forth certain viewpoints on the value of life. He outlines a doctrine of opposites, like two currents flowing between the same banks. Woven into the fabric of his music, Qoheleth asks a much larger, more persistent question about what is the worth of life? What real value does life have to offer? How do we come to grips with the mystery and ambiguity of life, those shadowy things that we can't fix but can only experience. Qoheleth confronts the big religious questions that have endured throughout human history, questions probably asked by the golfer, or the divorced friend who has difficulty seeing a promising future, or even the neighbor with small children who has lost her job. These days, we don't need to look too far to encounter some of the same doubts, and questions.

Eventually I made my way back from the East coast to Wisconsin where I stopped for a visit with my family before driving to my home in Saint Paul. The golfer's story continued to linger in my thoughts as I meandered along country roads. It was

Who Shall We Be?

a dazzling October day complete with clear skies, radiant maples, and shimmering red oaks. The fields stood naked of their grains. Farm tractors bumped over the unpaved roads hauling corn, soybeans and hay bales to their winter storage places. The familiar rural landscape stood quietly, waiting for the leaves to complete their cycle and become host to winter's softness. It also felt familiar and comforting after the horror and chaos of the previous weeks. Autumn was preparing for nature's last hurrah.

Yet shorter days and cooler nights also stir in us a sense of sadness. Just on the other side of color and clarity hides an edge of sorrow for having to bid goodbye to the passing summer. It caused me to reflect on all that I had witnessed in recent weeks, including the condition of our wounded world.

Autumn reveals both promising possibilities and limitations. It gives us natural beauty to love and stoke our memories in the winter darkness. Yet it also reveals some of the boundaries and truths of our lives. In late autumn we celebrate Halloween, which according to ancient mythology, marked the beginning of the sacred season when the gods came close and walked upon the earth.

Theologian Martin Marty in his book *Winter of the Heart* uses winter as a metaphor for wilderness. Though it might feel like a time and place in which God is the most absent, in fact,

God could be most present in our lives. In other words, God's presence can become even more compelling during long winter silences when we reflect on our lives. If autumn moves us toward the persistent human questions concerning the mystery of time, our relationships with one another, and the human search for that which endures, winter calls us to listen for God's reply.

In our quest for things of value, trusting in God or a higher power's goodness offers us many ideas – especially about the way we treat one another. Yet, faith does not remake the human condition. We do. Nor does faith undue human cruelty or disregard for life. We do. Faith, like it's partner hope, does not reshape the natural forces around us. Whether or not we believe, time continues to flow. Nature moves through her cycles. Faith changes nothing in the external world of fact but can transform everything in the inner world of the spirit. Faith enables us to see our lives within a larger landscape, connected to all others. Faith gives us life viewed from the vantage point of love.

Hope constitutes a key spiritual element of healing. Hope provides purpose, direction and a reason for being. I would add that hope is an attitude toward life, not just an occasional feeling we turn to when we need it. It is a disposition that says the future is an open one. It is a belief in future good.

Though I have no way of knowing whether the golfer in the Public Radio story moved forward into a current of hope, I suspect that his first steps to reestablish order to the chaotic events of the day included managing his bag of golf balls. Hopefully this activity propelled him toward other healing measures, within himself and beyond.

That morning, as I contemplated the golfer's behavior. I sensed that he was taking comfort in his simple activity. This suggested that his orderly process of selecting, preparing and striking a golf ball helped him regain his composure lost in the mayhem taking place across the river. He appeared to be replacing order in the face of chaos.

Over time, I have observed gravely ill hospital patients as well as friends and family members when their lives have run headlong into a crisis. The initial response typically includes chaos and confusion. Yet, once the emotions cool, I've also observed that healing and calm likely come through simple, uncomplicated practices. For example: early morning walks, with a trusted friend; a picnic in the back yard with favorite neighbors; a community garden for growing flowers and fresh vegetables; a glorious autumn drive down a country road. None of these activities requires a big investment of time or money. Yet, each offers the prospect of returning peace and order disrupted by chaos. The simple, inexpensive medicine can be powerful following a chaotic loss or misfortune.

Whether we are attempting to live and hope in a troubled world, or we have experienced a life-altering loss, it is wise to stop, eliminate as much turmoil as possible, and trust that the confusion will wane. On days when we simply do not understand the anger, violence, and polarization of our beloved country and the world around us, it's essential to seek out those things that endure. All the confusion, and disorder of life cannot stop Spring from reappearing.

So, how do we describe hope? I would portray it as a state of mind, not a state of the world. It's an ability to work for something simply because it is good. The message of hope is one that says renewal is always possible because life itself is always driven and supported by the forces of renewal. We don't have to figure out how to transform and renew our life. That knowledge and power is already there in nature, as any good Franciscan would say. We see this when we cut our finger in the garden, and it heals. We see it when the tulips and trilliums emerge, and redwing blackbirds return in the spring.

Hope provides an important spiritual component of healing. It offers purpose and direction, as well as a reason for being. Hope encompasses a type of faith that says we can transcend the present situation. It's a fundamental attitude toward life, not an individual life experience.

Who Shall We Be?

Hope is not just an occasional feeling we turn to when we need it. It is a disposition that says the future is an open one, and I can dare to believe it holds integrity. That future good can occur even in the face of loss or an unplanned change of direction and the struggles that go with it. Hope like faith engages our capacity to see ourselves in a larger landscape, a landscape in which we can experience God's healing opportunities that help us transcend the present situation, whatever that might be.

One could also describe hope as a light that shows us a new path. In my experience and that of patients and friends, this light can be informative and rewarding. It can also reveal a new or repurposed talent.

For example, several years ago, I experienced a string of upsets that resulted in a major shift in my life and a need to pursue something new. It began with the unexpected elimination of my job. This was followed by my son experiencing life- altering injuries in a motorcycle accident. Simultaneously, his gifted surgeon with whom I had become close friends died a mysterious and violent death. The cumulative effects caused by these three events left me feeling paralyzed. Yet, as I processed the chaos, I recalled several friends and acquaintances who had experienced comparable life altering setbacks. Each demonstrated a level of resilience and hope that enabled them to recreate a genuinely fulfilling life. My next thought was why not identify, interview, and publish a book featuring examples of these amazingly gifted and resilient "life rebuilders?"

Next, I set out to identify examples of this remarkable skill. Though this occurred before the onset of social media, it was not long before I gathered a list of extraordinary strangers from throughout the United States. My invitation to each person was this: First I would like to interview you about your journey. Then I invite you to share your name and contact information should a reader wish to connect with you.

Everyone agreed. *The Promise in Plan B," What We Bring To The Next Chapter Of Our Life* turned out to be as healing for me to write as for readers who discovered hope in the words. I learned that the process of exploring and harnessing our faith and creativity requires us to bravely hold the woundedness that surrounds us, rather than ignore it. Each person I interviewed, shared that their healing experience resulted in deeper bonds and radical interdependence upon their faith and upon one another.

When we find ourselves in the middle of a crisis or disruption resulting in life-altering loss, it is important to take time to grieve, rest, and regain our bearings. It is equally important to pay attention to that voice that keeps asking what matters most in our life? What do I need?

Who Shall We Be?

Grief and loss are not items we shop for. However, these unwelcomed guests manage to show up anyway. And it's not uncommon to get bogged down in them, or to ignore certain important messages in the experience. Instead, we might simply soldier through without making a thoughtful appraisal of how and why we feel pain. How might we adjust our path toward feeling whole and well?

The first stage of a crisis could find us "pulling down the shades and locking the doors: At this point, it is important to note that everyone heals differently. For example, it's easy to become cynical these days. Sometimes it feels as if the world is coming apart at the seams. I'm tired of the violence. I'm sick of my job. I didn't save enough money to retire. I just don't feel like celebrating or doing something new.

These might be perfectly true and very human responses to stress and disappointment but if joy is a goal, it's vital for us to remain in the game. We exude a powerful energy when we discover what matters most and how we can lead in our own space.

For example, I once accepted a job at a local garden center. I love gardening and truly missed the exquisite gardens from my previous home. Little did I expect that the garden center job would create an opportunity for me to share this gift of nurturing plants. They invited me to help children and adults who had experienced a serious losses learn how to garden.

This kind of opportunity reminds me that all of us are the authors of our lives. This means that even in the face of cynicism and loss, we must get on the train to new ways of thinking and celebrating life. We can be a leavening agent. Like yeast raising bread, we can breathe new energy into our homes, our neighborhoods, jobs and places of worship.

However, it will come as no surprise that a commitment like this might require adjusting our personal reality. Each of us is a product of our own unique history, including our attitudes, beliefs, and what we've grown up with or grown accustomed to over time. What feels comfortable or what does not? When we think about the degree of joy we experience or don't experience, we need to think about the source of our beliefs. Who or what shaped our beliefs? Did someone teach me? Did I accept them by default? Through marriage? Careers? Have I ever gone back to check out these beliefs, feelings and attitudes for their effectiveness? Remember that joy is about making peace with who we are (my authentic self), Why we are (how did I become this self?) and how we are (how do I choose to experience life going forward?)

We are the authors of our story, and this story will likely change in the face of setbacks, attitudes and responses to life.

Who Shall We Be?

In the words of author and teacher Joseph Campbell, "The privilege of a lifetime is being who you are.

The Power of Story

Forty-one years immersed in the role of chaplain has found me occasionally fielding questions such as, "Why would anyone choose a professional path like this? Why would anyone willingly walk into the lives of others at chaotic, often miserable moments, including unthinkable loss?

Having given these questions plenty of thought, my only answer can be, because we need one another. We need one another in our celebrations and in our losses. We need one another to share and listen to each of our stories, our questions, our joys and sorrows, and our dreams.

Let me tell you a little story that might explain my choice to tackle chaos and pain for a living. Perhaps this brief account simply proves that I'm impulsive and reckless. Perhaps I'm a little of each.

I've always loved birds. My mother made certain that my brother and I knew a robin from a rose breasted grossbeak before we were ten years old. It was not uncommon for her to awaken us at four A.M. to head for a swamp where we would count sandhill cranes for the Audubon Society. We also were responsible for cleaning bird baths and feeding chickadees and hummingbirds in the back yard. I still walk around with a Peterson Bird Guide in my pocket. My dog and I love hiking the Dakota Trail near my home, as well as the Gunflint Trail and Superior National Forest. This is where we enjoy identifying everything from white throated sparrows to eagles, ravens, hawks and owls.

So, not long ago during the Christmas holiday I was walking my dog through our neighborhood when we encountered a piercing shriek from a very large hawk. A red shouldered hawk to be exact. This hefty and angry fellow was tangled in bird netting, plus holiday lights that had been draped over shrubs to protect small birds.

As startling as it was to come face to face with this handsome guy, I impulsively grabbed and held on to him until he calmed down. He was, indeed, a Red Shouldered male. His size alone left the dog and me seriously questioning my impulsive move to save his life.

Next began the task of extracting the hawk from this mess. Unfortunately, we failed at that as well. Finally, with seemingly no other options, I ripped the entire mess of netting and lights off the shrubs, and the three of us, dog, bird, and reckless woman set out to find some help. We must have presented quite a picture for the neighbors-- a disheveled woman, a leaping and barking dog, a very large bird, and a mess of lights and netting.

Eventually we came to a neighbor's open garage where I called in to see if anyone could help- or at least bring me scissors. Fortunately, someone heard my shouts, and a woman rushed out with what looked like surgical scissors. The two of us exchanged a brief hello and went to work.

Who Shall We Be?

It took us nearly an hour. I managed the "patient," turning him and opening his wings to enable the neighbor to get under his feathers. Even his talons were wrapped in netting. What a prison he had landed in. Through all this mashing and maneuvering the hawk never struggled. He never made a sound. This formidable predator simply watched quietly with seemingly a sense of knowing we would not hurt him. Even as I warned the woman to keep her face away from the bird's talons, she ignored my warning, and the hawk never became aggressive. Piece by piece we separated him from the trap he had landed in. Finally, when we were finished and had examined the bird for any injuries, I stepped outside of the garage, opened my hands and watched this magnificent guy fly up over the rooftops.

I must admit this entire experience has continued to live in my thoughts. It was a profoundly moving event that felt much bigger than a bird watching two women with scissors. It felt like a metaphor, an image of a larger truth of cutting through the nets that separate us in our wounded, polarized world. I am also reminded that hawks are fearsome predators. They take no prisoners when they're out hunting. They are swift, agile, strong, and relentless. Additionally, they enjoy a long history as wisdom figures among indigenous tribes and beyond.

If this was indeed a metaphor, I believe that truth is about how we all need one another. We need one another in our mourning; in our problem solving; in our celebrations; in our listening and education. We need one another in our story telling and reconciliation, and in our willingness to sacrifice on behalf of ourselves and others. I further believe that this truth is about how we heal when we share our stories with one another.

Yet, like my hawk, we've been confined in ways that have tested our ability to break free. Anger, distrust, racism and more have too often stood in the way of respect and kindness. It hasn't mattered how gifted, capable, wealthy, or powerful we are, we simply can't go it alone. None of these qualities keep us from getting sick, or from losing our homes in wildfires or tornados. None of these qualities guarantee we won't lose our job or our life savings. We need one another. We need community, not chaos.

As we hope against hope that we are nearing the end of this chapter of angst and cynicism within our own country and elsewhere, we must ask ourselves, "Who shall we be?" I believe we are called to be a beloved community. When I say beloved, I'm not speaking of sentimental, naïve love. I'm speaking of the kind of love that seeks the good for others as well as for us. I'm speaking of the Nelson Mandela, Archbishop Desmond Tutu kind of love. Both men have sacrificed their lives to do what is right and merciful. They knew this was the only way to heal a wounded country.

Who Shall We Be?

This brings me back to my earlier question of "Why would anybody make a career (such as mine) of wading into another's miserable experience. Why would we want to hear other's stories?

My experience tells me that it has never been about "fixing" or offering magical solutions with perfect endings when life has taken a difficult turn. It has been about deeply listening to another's stories. There is nothing complicated about listening, though it does require that we stop talking. I would call listening to one another's stories an instrument of peace. Nothing magical but a willingness to create a space from which another can discover "Who shall I be?"

Speaking of listening to other's stories, I recently attended a funeral for a well-known and well-loved man in my small-town community. This fellow had built a widely popular garden business and was known as generous, funny, fair and kind. His parents had also built a storied dime store business that people still rave about. They too enjoyed a reputation for kindness and community engagement.

Though this man's painful death had left friends and family heartbroken, hundreds showed up to honor him at a lovely funeral. Then, as the service came to an end, the minister invited members of the congregation to briefly share their memories of their dear friend. They did just that. However, they did not simply share their sorrows and sense of loss. Instead, they burst into laughter describing wild fishing trips, embarrassing blind dates, silly parenting episodes, family picnics, and more. I would describe it as heart felt exchange of joyful life stories and events with their friend as truly healing for everyone. In fact, the mood shifted from sadness to a joyful celebration of life together.

In the end, I felt heartened at the minister's recognition that all our stories are valuable. This includes our accounts of losses, illnesses, and happy triumphs. These are the episodes and experiences that shape us and make us who we are. Each of our lives includes stories of loss, learning, and disruption, as well as accounts of joy. These are the narratives that make us who we are. I believe that listening to our own stories as well as those of others truly matters. Whether it's a sorrowful tale of illness or a jubilant account of a new baby's birth, all of it matters, and we all benefit and grow when we listen.

Belonging Nurtures Personal and Community Wellbeing

"I find hope in the darkest of days and focus on the brightness. I do not judge the universe.

Dalai Lama

When a patient or family facing a health crisis asks me a question such as, "Why? How did this happen? "Why me?" Or, "What does this mean?" I know that we are about to have a conversation about God or a Higher Power.

This was what I witnessed when a physician friend invited me to join him for a meeting at the local gospel mission. It was an evening discussion with individuals defined as late-stage alcoholics. Most were homeless and had been living, or perhaps only surviving, without benefit of any sort of community or even the support of friends.

When we entered the room, the small circle of homeless men was listening attentively as their counselor announced the weekly assignment. The faces might have belonged to anyone anywhere. They consisted of professionals with postgraduate degrees to the old and sickly. They had come to the gospel mission from offices and street corners, jails and reservations. They called themselves chronic alcoholics, the men who huddle beneath bridges in the December cold sipping kerosene. Many had gone again and again through local detox centers and shelters. All were searching for a welcoming community and a reason to hope.

The counselor had just asked them to write another weekly prayer to be discussed at the next meeting. It appeared that everyone was managing to cobble together some prayerful words to share with the group. That is, everyone except an older fellow who sat in a corner of the room by himself. Each time the counselor asked how he was coming along with the assignment, he simply shook his head. Years on the streets, immersed in alcohol and gloom, had left him empty and alone.

My physician friend and I learned that several weeks had passed, during which the other group members had been discussing their stories and prayers. It was clear to both of us that these fellows also benefited from a sense of community and trust.

On the evening of our third weekly visit, the ragged group assembled once more, and the counselor again asked the reluctant fellow if he brought his prayer.

"Yes" was the reply, much to everyone's surprise. He then pulled a crumbled bit of paper from his pocket and recited a six-word entreaty: "Whoever made me, keep me safe."

The substance of his petition disclosed so much about the person who prayed it. For me, it revealed that, at the core of every human being who faces a crisis, burns a soul searching for healing and support of others. This healing likely begins with a connection to a community, or source of strength and goodness beyond self. In this case the healing included a powerful, bond of trust within a group of wounded souls. Some would call this a spiritual search and discovery of authentic community and connection. For the once isolated man, it demonstrated what it meant to belong.

So, why does belonging matter? Spirituality is a popular concept, mentioned over and over in today's self-help and whole body-medicine literature. Yet, spiritual language continues to be confined to recovery and religious communities. We often read about all the things a person can do to improve his or her spiritual health, but rarely do we talk about what it means to be a spiritually whole person. In fact, even though spirituality lies at the heart of AA's Twelve steps and most world religions, it's not often pointed out that the Twelve Steps of AA simply provide one means of nurturing spiritual growth.

At first glance, the idea of belonging seems like a logical and perhaps simple goal. Yet, the invasion of a world changing pandemic followed by a country-wide eruption of anger, political polarization and racism has marked a troubling point in our country's history. In addition to the loss of lives and, in some cases, overall wellbeing, these dramatic historical events have also influenced our feelings about trust, partnerships and seriously belonging. On one hand we continue to belong to churches, support groups, work groups, book clubs, and professional organizations. On the other hand, worries about spreading disease through group gatherings, distrust of other's motives, and confidence in our ability to "go it alone," suggest that we have lost some of our interest in belonging. This climate of doubt also adds to a sense of isolation that can disrupt our work and personal connections to friends and family. We are likely to find ourselves looking deeply into our own stories for signs and direction. Where are we? Do we feel "a part of?" Do we possess the resources to connect deeply with one another, in community or must we go looking for new resources.

Who Shall We Be?

A culture of shifting landscapes, and diminishing guideposts also contributes to a climate of chronic insecurity. All of this can add to a sense of isolation by disrupting our work and personal connections to friends and family. We find ourselves looking deeply into our own stories for signs and direction. Where are we? Do we feel "a part of"? Do we still possess the resources to connect deeply with one another, in community, or must we go looking for these resources?

My professional path has been one of listening to people talk about their lives—their dreams, their losses, and yes, their unmet needs to belong. My work typically begins with attending to someone's human story. These stories speak of sickness and health. They describe success and failure, recovery and death. They touch every possibility, and a few seemingly impossibilities, that folks carry with them. They embrace virtually every social, economic, and cultural experience one can imagine. Yet, while these stories differ widely in their circumstances, they often share a theme: the problem of belonging or, perhaps more accurately, the problem of not belonging.

The answer, I believe, is yes, we do have the resources. No, we do not have to look beyond ourselves for them. However, to tap the wellspring of intimacy, a quality of belonging, requires commitment, nurture, and maybe even a change of heart. There are simply no quick fixes and no easy answers to fill this need of belonging. Ultimately there is no path except the path made by our own walking, our humanity and our inherent human skill to be our brother's keeper. Through this, we learn about our extraordinary ability to create a sense of community and place for ourselves and others. We begin to see every-day experiences and relationships in new ways, as rich sources of vitality and sustenance.

Belonging takes work. It sometimes means refashioning our communities on the job and at home. It could mean rediscovering the value of friendships, mentors, and healing capacity of wasting time wisely with those we care about. Belonging also means including those who are alone. Whether we are speaking about our homes, schools, workplace, churches, and beyond, to belong to a community is to move in the direction of the larger whole. This gift is not simply a focus on our own goals and objectives. Belonging to a community invites the kind of inclusiveness that likely results in wellbeing and being well.

Each of us as a distinct and separate person possess a sense of isolation, of living within the boundaries of the self. Yet we also have a basic need to believe that we belong in the world in some meaningful way. We inherently understand that we can transcend our separate selves. In part, the term "spirituality" is used to address this universal human longing for intimacy and community. To be spiritually whole means we have examined central issues of life, such as our understanding of ourselves and how we relate to others and the world we live in.

The spiritual dimension is difficult to define, let alone measure. It does not meet the objective criteria needed for scientific analysis. To some, its subjective manifestations might seem to involve wishful thinking, pathological projection, or the abandonment of rational analysis. Because of this, the spiritual dimension of health has not always enjoyed a highly valued place in the medical world.

In fact, the term "spirituality" is applied mainly to subjective phenomena. There are several concepts, however, that help capture some elements of spirituality. The following encompass some, though not all.

A belief in some intrinsic meaning or order in the universe

A faith that humanity and creation are inherently good

An understanding that the force hidden in creation is a loving, present and active energy

A trust that this active energy behind creation could be called God or a Higher Power

A willingness to accept what is, which is not to be confused with grudging resignation or with approval of evil

A fundamental expectation of future good

An ability to find peace of mind in an imperfect, ambiguous world

A capacity to make peace with the knowledge that one's own personality is imperfect, although acceptable.

Recently I experienced an event that demonstrated a genuine expression of welcome and trust, qualities that invite belonging. The circumstances involved the death of a beloved member of our congregation. We were told that this would be a large funeral. Fortunately, an equally large group of church members offered to help. This help included everything from cleaning, baking, moving furniture, setting up a family room complete with fruit, cookies, coffee, lunch preparation, and a big video screen for sharing family history and photos. The choir and organist practiced family favorite music. A bishop and dear family friend traveled from South Carolina to preside at the service.

My role and that of a priest friend involved welcoming guests as they arrived. We did so by holding the front doors open, offering a welcoming handshake, and guiding each adult and child to the guest book, name tags, restrooms, and a place to hang their coats. The reception area quickly erupted into everything from tears to laughter, warm embraces and galloping children greeting their friends. It felt like a true celebration of a beloved one's life.

Who Shall We Be?

The service continued to maintain a celebratory tone. The selection of music, the eulogy, the sermon, and guest participation spoke lovingly in appreciation for this delightful father and grandfather. The service ended with a promise of grandpas favorite ice cream bars following lunch.

All of this reminded me that hope and joy constitute key elements of spiritual growth and healing. Hope provides purpose, direction, and a reason for being. It encompasses an assured sense that we can transcend the present situation whatever that might be. It's a fundamental attitude toward life, an attitude that flourishes when we belong. It appeared to me that each guest and those who prepared for and participated in the funeral felt the same.

It would not surprise me if some of those funeral guests would return to our church to see if it might be a place to belong.

Not Belonging Invites Isolation and Loneliness

Socially isolated individuals occasionally share with me that they do not feel cared for, valued or esteemed. They also tend to lack a sense of belonging and sustenance that a social support system provides.

Who Shall We Be?

Years ago, my brother convinced my parents to celebrate Christmas on Christmas Eve. In previous years we had opened gifts and enjoyed our festive meal on Christmas Day. If I am correct, my mother also tampered with the menu that year, substituting jellied cranberry sauce for the whole berries. With best intensions, she might have placed the tree in a different location to free up the living room fireplace.

For the next decade, every member of our family talked about the year my mother ruined Christmas. A woman who had never intentionally done an unkind thing had dared to change a few old traditions, not even particularly good ones. Nobody was about to let her forget her indiscretion.

Change, especially changing the way we've always done things, troubles most of us. Change can be as simple as adjusting to daylight saving time or as complex as gaining a new perspective on racial, social, or political matters. In any case, change threatens to destroy the shield that protects our security. It sends up red flags of discomfort and leaves us feeling faintly unsettled or, in some cases, paralyzed. But change can often point us toward a new doorway to wholeness. Our ability or lack of ability to alter attitudes and routines determines the quality of everything from our careers to our personal relationships, from our problem- solving skills to our spiritual growth.

I'm convinced that few of us choose to change much. Instead, we tend to move somewhat grudgingly, with the flow, making necessary adjustments along the way. Rarely do we resist like the woman I have known who simply said no, and then retreated to an empty house on a remote hilltop near a farm where I boarded my horse. At ninety- four years old, she had no intention of changing anything, including her cloistered lifestyle. Living with other people would require more adjustments than she was willing to make. Instead, she chose a life of isolation.

Florence Sedwick lived in the hills of western Wisconsin. Over the decades, she withdrew from her small farming community. Only an occasional bit of gossip reminded residents that she ever lived there. Jason Baur from the Mondovi Co-op Equity claimed she buried a fortune under her hay shed. A butcher in Bob's IGA insisted that she was once committed to a mental institution. A world War I veteran in the local nursing home said she set fire to a bunkhouse up the valley on the Werlein farm, a fire that killed her supposedly philandering husband. Nevertheless, after years of speculation, nobody really knew much about Florence, or Flossy, as she chose to be called. All this struck me as curious, because the ramshackle, unpainted fortress where she lived was only a few miles west of town.

No photos or records of her existed in the local library. No letters or church archives held a reliable history of her. The unkempt footpath leading to her front door testified that nobody came to call. She lived a solitary existence, a hermit who aroused only a modest ripple of curiosity. A few enterprising journalists once tried to interview her for a feature in the local newspaper, but they found themselves looking down the business end of a twelve-gauge shotgun. To the best of everyone's knowledge, they never went back.

Concerning the mysterious space of her hermitage, the bizarre tales proliferated. Hence, I seriously questioned my judgement on that June morning when I rode my horse up the lane to her house. The early sun slanted through an old apple orchard, the trees like broken sentries guarding the entrance to her property. A first cutting of hat lay in damp windrows beneath the ground fog. Cows and their calves traversed the hillside to rejoin one another after a night spent scattered throughout the pasture. We passed an abandoned cottage where O'Malley's hired man, Mel Jacobson used to live. The cats had taken charge ever since Mel had a stroke and moved to the Valley

Nursing home in Durand. A litter of kittens tumbled off the front stoop into a neglected bed of daylilies.

I might not have seen her if she hadn't frightened my horse, causing him to vault up the embankment. By anybody's standards, she was an awesome sight, a wizened gnome stooped in the tall grass. She clutched the handle of a doubled-bladed ax. Her expression hovered between anger and interest. She crouched, poised for combat. Oddly she wore a dress. Odder still, the dress was secured with large safety pins to several layers of long underwear. Her leathery skin hung about her neck and over her muscular arms. She had immense hands that looked as if they belonged to a man. A pink plastic barrette held her hair off her forehead, and a plain wedding band and wire-rimmed spectacles offered the only clues that she had ever known human contact.

My horse was, by now, hopelessly unmanageable. I had to dismount or be thrown. Choosing the first option, I slipped out of the saddle and stood about a dozen feet from the old woman. She gripped her ax but didn't make any threatening moves, nor did she run away. A long moment passed before it occurred to me to offer my hand in a greeting. Surprisingly she stepped forward, shook my extended hand, and began to talk about my horse's behavior.

Who Shall We Be?

"I'm not surprised he's afeared of me," she announced simply. "Dogs is too. It's because I'm too old. I've lived too long. But my cat Jefferson back home... Well, now that a different story. He loves me. Never leaves home for longer than a day. He stays to home the way he should.

I soon learned that Flossy was born on a small farm in the nearby township of Dover. "Three generations of us have growed up right in this here area," she explained. "My mother was born in a log cabin on the hill behind my place. This is home for me. I'd rather take a pounding than go to town. As far as I'm concerned, I'll be here on my forty for three hundred and sixty-five days a year till the day I die."

Eccentric or not, Flossy had something in common with any of us who ever wanted to run away from the pain and responsibility of living with others. The primary difference in Flossie was that she never mastered the art of adapting to change. The losses and setbacks that most people experience in a lifetime drove her in a different direction. Through the years, she slowly withdrew, finally choosing to make her journey alone rather than risk any more losses or adjustments.

Flossy and her husband, "the Old Gent," began farming their plot in 1920. "We worked with the neighbors back then" she said, especially when we were threshing or shredding. I had my own beautiful team, Florie Bay and Ted. Them and me hauled grain shocks out of the field all day long. After the bundles dried, I'd run the steam thresher to separate the grain from the straw. I've never driven a car, but I can drive any horse or steam engine you could find me."

Flossie chose her own road and then walked it... alone. As she grouped through her memories of cooking and harvesting, I could see how each bit of past misfortune had nudged her further from the company of others. During our subsequent visits she created for me a patchwork account of her history: the Depression, crop loss, and the Old Gent's death. Then her children left home, automated methods of farming took over, followed by a legal battle to keep her beloved forty. Faced with seemingly endless difficult decisions, she focused on the only thing she felt she had left—her homestead. "I made up my mind long ago I would rally here or perish," she said. "It's quiet here and it's mine."

There Flossy remained, spending most of her hours collecting fruits and nuts, chopping brush and splitting firewood for her Heaterolla stove. Every summer a local mill delivered ten loads of wood. By fall, she has cut and neatly stacked each piece behind her back porch. Now and then, someone drops off food and other staples at her mailbox. She loads the supplies into a wheelbarrow and pushes it up the half-mile hill. Jars of canned meats and fruits fill her pantry shelf, and large bowls of hand pumped water line the countertop. Rags provide curtains for the open windows, and braided rags are scattered on the unfinished wood floor. In a wooden crate next to the pump house sleeps her only companion, Jefferson.

Flossie's story was both troubling and seductive. I saw something deliciously alluring about the idea of vanishing, of casting off the complicated relationships and demanding commitments that sap me of energy. Nevertheless, Flossie also wore the unmistakable signs of estrangement and sadness that accompany a choice to retreat from community. Though she spoke with enthusiasm about her life on the forty, I sensed a hollowness in her spirit and a longing for human contact that had nothing to do with her age.

Most of the locals were satisfied to call Flossie crazy, but her desire to escape is far from unique. Scores of people race through life, paying it little more than a courtesy call; they're visitors and sightseers instead of pilgrims. Consider how many friends are injured by divorce and never choose intimacy again.

Think of those who remain stuck in insufferable jobs and abusive relationships. In fact, a large segment of the human race views success as something that comes only when we bolt down the hatches and secure all aspects of our lives into predictable patterns of sameness, efficiency, and stability.

Success as I've grown to understand it cannot be measured by what one is or does, but only by distance traveled. We are forever moving from one experience to another, one challenge to another, one relationship, one loss or achievement to another. We are unfinished business, shaped and reshaped by our continuing experience. It is this fluid and changing quality of life that invites us to become resilient rather than resistant, to belong rather than to retreat. Openness and a receptive heart clear the way for more adventure. To be open means to make ourselves available to life, particularly life in community with others. Openness allows us to drop our past rebuffs, rejections, and retreats, our victories and our failures. It helps us see things afresh, as always newborn and stocked with possibilities. The challenge to become so open to life that nothing can destroy us.

The ability to handle change and stay connected is a learned gift. It often demands many alterations in the original plan. These changes pull us out of our secure little niches and place us in unfamiliar territory. We instinctively want security,

Who Shall We Be?

even if that security is an unpleasant repetition of past mistakes. The learning comes in letting go of some of the controls we tend to apply. The rewards come with discovering those things that we might have missed through our own refusal to consider a new way.

Nowhere are there any written guarantees that things will work out comfortably for us. Yet joy comes from our ability to transform and grow together with others regardless of discomfort and ambiguity. We gain nothing by pulling down the blinds or by giving way to cynicism and despair.

How sad it would be for us to go to the kitchen one morning and find that there was no bread. How very sad it would be if we were to go to the kitchen and find that we were not hungry.

Looking for Meaning

One in creation, you and I
Kindred spirits
Beloved
And bounded together
Untouched
By a world of limitations
Walking together

Who Shall We Be?

Upon the holy ground
Of shared experience
Knowing
We are human
And
This is enough

Years ago, early in my chaplaincy experience, I received a message to come to labor and delivery. It was late afternoon, nearing a shift change. The social worker had just interviewed the Robinson family and felt they might benefit from a pastoral presence. Though the Robinsons did n not belong to a local church, Mr. Robinson expressed a curiosity about meeting a woman minister.

"Mom is clearly full term, and her baby has died," reported the social worker, highlighting some of the pertinent details in Mrs. Robinson's chart. "She also has three small children at home and probably suffers from serious psychiatric problems, she mumbled offhandedly. Maybe bipolar disorder, schizophrenia, or borderline personality. The woman's reaction to her baby's death seemed "flat," according to others present at the nursing station. Most of the staff agreed that Mrs. Robinson had been joking oddly and that she failed to grasp the meaning of what was taking place in her life and her body.

A discussion then ensued about Mrs. Robinson's intellectual competence. The staff had given her some printed material about grief and loss, though they couldn't tell if she understood it, or even cared. Perhaps the loss of this child was a relief to her, given the fact that she had a brood of very young at home. The nurses and case managers continued to speculate about the situation. An unspoken question underlay their discussion: "Why would the Robinsons continue to have children when Mrs. Robinson was so ill and already had three youngsters.

I also wondered about the entire incident, as I observed the facial expressions around me. The expressions denoted everything from bewilderment to hostility and self-righteousness.

"How about the baby's father?" I asked. "Is he here?"

He was. According to the staff, Mr. Robinson was behaving strangely, as well. His strident voice and peculiar jokes made them uneasy. He dominated his wife, bossing her and hardly permitting her to answer questions for herself. Troubling, too, were his constant references to what he called his wife's medical mismanagement. He clearly thought that this might have contributed to their baby's death and his questions were having a chilling effect on the various health professionals engaged in his wife's care.

Who Shall We Be?

Yet, though overbearing and odd, Mr. Robinson appeared quite supportive of his wife-- quite sympathetic and reassuring. As I listened to the cacophony of opinions about the couple, it struck me that they were just that -- individual opinions reflecting individual preferences, experiences, and comfort levels. The final diagnosis: Mr. Robinson talked too much, and he was... well she was...that is, they were different. The social worker nodded in agreement

I soon learned that the Robinsons were, indeed, different. They differed from me and from the rest of the staff in ways that hindered much meaningful contact. While the differences began at a racial level, they included profound social, cultural, educational, and financial contrasts. The Robinsons embodied what could be described as a subculture of loss. White, middle-class, and educated, the rest of us exemplified a culture of privilege beyond the Robinson's experience or even comprehension.

The idea of being privileged did not automatically jump off my tongue. At that point in my history, I might have described myself as neutral or benign. To my knowledge, I had never intentionally wielded power over others. Nothing in my upbringing or education gave me any training in seeing myself as an oppressor. In fact, peace and social justice had already found my list of priorities and have remained core values that continue to shape my pastoral ministry. I also know that I spend most of my waking moments in the company of other whites, a relatively easy audience for me to identify and negotiate. In addition, I possess a convenient little bundle of provisions, or tools that make my life uncommonly palatable -- a passport, checkbook, credit cards, a home, a car that runs, health insurance, and perhaps the most significant, choices. This kind of privilege has little to do with my good intensions. A lifetime of good intensions did not make me any less privileged in the eyes of the people I was about to meet.

Mr. Robinson greeted me loudly with a predictable remark about never having met a lady preacher. A thin veneer of jolly chatter barely concealed his anxiety and confusion. It wasn't long before he got to the point of his concern. "They say that our baby be dead for a long time," he announced. "Maybe a month. Maybe it plans on risen up like Lazarus! Do you think so, Reverend?"

He slapped his knee and, with a loud guffaw, beckoned to his wife, evidently granting her permission to chuckle with him over his icebreaking joke. She lay quietly in the bed staring out the window, uncommitted to a discussion of any type. Mr. Robinson veered from one unrelated topic to another regaling me with stories about everything from his tour of duty in the U.S. Army to the theology of Martin Luther.

Who Shall We Be?

I asked if they had friends that I could call for them. "No," he replied. "We keep pretty much to ourselves. I maybe leave the house to go to the grocery store, but I don't stay away long. We stick with each other and our kids most the time."

"How about family?" I pressed, hoping to identify someone who might lend support. Mr. Robinson's parents had died some time ago. Mrs. Robinson's mother lived in Arkansas, but didn't have a telephone -- or much else. Neither of them knew how to reach any relatives.

"No, we don't need to call no family," said Mr. Robinson. "We can take care of this ourselves."

Soon I learned that the Robinsons had left Arkansas six months ago. They were heading for Canada when their dilapidated car broke down on the freeway. A highway patrolman arrived and, upon discovering that they had no automobile insurance, collected a $300 fine from them. The encounter left the family broke and marooned in the Twin Cities. When we met, they had already moved several times in search of a safe neighborhood for their children.

"A baby always loves you, you know," whispered Mrs. Robinson. "Like, I know that a baby needs me to take care of it. I like that, don't you? I'm scared."

"A lady preacher. Well now ain't that something? It would be good if you stayed with my wife while she has that baby. You know my sister lost a baby once, And my wife's mama lost twins. Hell, we've lost a lot of children, now that I think about it. Yes, you could be a comfort to her when she has that baby."

Loss of power. Loss of identity. Loss of life.

"Is there anyone you would like to see, or anything I could do for you? I've never had a child die. I don't know what it's like to be who you are or where you are. I'm so sorry."

"That baby ain't never done nonthin' wrong, has it? God is gonna welcome that baby, isn't He? 'Course He will. I know it couldn't be no other way. I mean what's that baby ever done wrong anyhow? Course God is gonna do that."

Loss of dignity. Loss of hope. Loss of dreams.

"You know, the other day I come out to get the car and the horn started to honk. Just like that. It was the day my wife learned that the baby died. That darn horn be honking all the way downtown. People kep' lookin at me, and I kep' holdin my hands up in the air-- like this--so they could see I wasn't doin' it myself. It was doin' it itself. Craziest thing I ever did see. I think maybe that baby's spirit was right in that car, don't you know? That be it. I know it. That baby's spirit was in that car telling us it was gonna be just fine up there in heaven. Do you think so, Reverend?"

Loss of access. Loss of privacy. Loss of connection.

Who Shall We Be?

"MR. Robinson, I was wondering if the three of us could hold hands for a few minutes."

He struggled out of his chair and made his way to the bedside where he took his wife's hand and then mine. We stood motionless against a backdrop of fetal monitors and rush-hour traffic. Gripped by my own inadequacy, I offered a halting prayer of encouragement… for all of us. Tears slowly slipped down Mr. Robinsons cheeks. Mrs. Robinson kept her silent vigil, seemingly trying to summon the courage to give birth to her dead child.

We tightened our grips on one another's hands, a spontaneous gesture that found me at once understanding everything and nothing.

It was but a mere hesitation, a suspended moment in space when we three said yes to a life shared and broken. Wordlessly we acknowledged the fragile and precious thread that knitted us together, suspended in time and creation, a merging of kindred spirits never to be separated by a world of human limitations.

Mary Farr

Leading With Love

"No one listens," they tell me, and so I listen… and I tell them what they have just told me, and I sit in silence, listening to them, letting them grieve. "Julian, you are wise," they say. "You have been gifted with understanding." And all I did was listen, for I believe full surely that God's spirit is in us all."

Who Shall We Be?

Julian of Norwich
Thirteenth-century English mystic

Listening means everything when it comes to health and wellbeing. While it plays an essential role in medicine, it also lies at the heart of justice, love, and peace. Our need to listen is surpassed only by our need to connect with one another and walk together on the holy ground of our human experience.

Years working in health care settings with health care professionals have also taught me that listening lies at the heart of justice, love, and peace. Our need to listen is surpassed only by our need to connect with one another and walk together on the holy ground of our human experience. This no doubt explains why long before my ordination to a servant ministry, I chose hospital chaplaincy as my vocational call. Specifically, I chose to engage in love's work in real people's lives.

Additionally, I understand that health and wholeness require much more than repaired body systems. In fact, I would suggest that complete healing happens at the level of soul. And when people ask me, "Where is God in today's newspaper reports of daily violence and apathy? Or, what is God's role in sickness and death? my answer can only be that the God I know is right here, in the faces and hands of those we encounter every day. The faith I embrace does not consist of a belief that we will be rescued from disease or death. It consists of a belief that we are loved, and no amount of suffering or illness can diminish our value and purpose in this world. Each of us is incredibly important. We have a story to tell as well as a need to listen – especially when it comes to being well and whole. I believe this is true whether we are at the giving or receiving end of care.

Speaking of listening, a single word kept coming up as I made this choice of a chaplaincy vocation: discernment. Discernment is larger than a time out to decipher the path ahead. It's a process that awaits thoughtful examination, information gathering, and judgment. This kind of discernment is also likely to follow a loss or uninvited life-change. Hence, it likely includes some anxiety.

In my case, three foundational experiences shaped this call. The first was an early introduction through the Episcopal Church to the International Order of Saint Luke the Physician. This healing ministry of clergy and laity is based on the belief that Holy Scriptures set forth healing as a continuing and essential part of the ministry committed to the church by Jesus Christ.

Who Shall We Be?

The second impetus came from my immersion in Clinical Pastoral Education, CPE. This provided an essential foundation that has supported me in a variety of settings, including adult, nursing home, and pediatric care settings.

The third driving force has been a longstanding commitment to my baptismal vows, particularly the vow that says, "I will strive for justice and peace among all people and respect the dignity of every human being."

Years serving in health care settings, listening to patients and their loved ones has taught me a great deal about the power of loss, as well as the potential for healing. Our life journeys consist of all sorts of turning points and passages. These passages become our personal stories of faith and hope. They are the tests and trials that shape and reshape us.

Each of these influences has also impacted my desire to love and serve by offering a welcoming, faith-filled presence to health care professionals, children, families, and communities seeking reconciliation or simply to be heard. Yet, a sensible person might ask why would someone choose a professional path like this? Why would anyone willingly spend years walking hospital hallways, intensive care units, and emergency rooms.?

Why would anyone wish to walk into the lives of others at such chaotic and miserable times? Isn't that obtrusive? Or maybe even foolish?

Reflecting on these experiences, I'm reminded of a conversation I had with the medical director of our hospital's newborn intensive care department. This is a department in which tiny, premature newborns and gravely ill babies tend to languish for long and stressful pieces of time. It's a tense experience for everyone including doctors, nurses, families and friends. When I asked him what he expected of our chaplains visiting the department, he replied simply, "I expect you to show up, listen, and tell the truth." This advice has proven to be a powerful affirmation of patients, families, and those who care for them. I have also observed that they invite a God presence and healing of the soul.

For example, an on- call chaplain showing up to visit a sick patient sounds like a perfectly reasonable expectation. Yet, the thought of heading home after an exhausting day visiting families and patients also sounds appealing. These were my thoughts one early morning after having spent the previous night in the hospital with a family whose child was in surgery. It was seven a.m. when I received a request for a visit from an eight-year-old boy with leukemia. He had come to the hospital to receive palliative care, as he was no longer a candidate for treatment.

Wearily I hiked up the stairs and found the boy in bed playing a card game. After introducing myself, I walked closer to the bed and shook his hand. He seemed pleased to have company. Though I never mentioned being in the hospital all night, he looked me over as closely as my mother might have when I came home late. That was when I asked him, "How could the two of us together make your day a good one?" Without hesitation, he said, "I would like to start it by saying a prayer for you." It was a prayer that I've never forgotten.

The second directive offered by the neonatologist can be life-changing for patients, families, and members of the entire care team. Listening. It's a foundational skill essential for all chaplains. yet, listening attentively to a someone's emotional needs is not easy. We tend to be a culture of "fixers." When things go wrong, we have a habit of sharing lots of ideas of how to make things go right. Though well-meaning friends and family members might be tempted to surround a patient with a suitcase full of solutions and directives, this is not always helpful.

For example, I once visited a young mother who had just lost her baby during her delivery. As I entered the room filled with well-intentioned friends and relatives, I heard a woman say to the grieving mother, "Oh, Louise, you are a young, healthy woman. You just need to forget all this and go home and get pregnant again. To the contrary, quietly listening to the mother's needs, would likely have benefited by a supportive prayer and a reminder that her friends will be there when she needs them.

The third pastoral value offered by the neonatologist—tell the truth, applies to each member of a care team. Sometimes a medical crisis brings many people to the site. Doctors, nurses, custodians, medical techs, family members and others likely show up when an emergency room event involves someone for whom they have provided care. When this happens, a chaplain must be a skilled pastor of people and groups. This chaplain must also be self-aware of his or her ministry and how it impacts others, including patients, families, and team members.

Such an event occurred in the emergency room in the hospital where I worked. Parents of a baby diagnosed with sudden infant death syndrome rushed into the hospital with their unconscious child. The care team, who had become familiar with the family immediately went to work. The room began to fill with concerned others who had provided care for the mother's late-in-life pregnancy. In this case, the care was not successful. The heartbreaking truth was the team was not able to save the baby.

A painful silence followed before the father turned to me and asked if he could baptize his baby boy. "Yes," was my answer, and I rushed off to get everything he needed for the baptism. He then took his wife's hand and thanked her for the blessing of their life together. I held the prayer book for him, as he gently baptized the child, then lifted him high above his head and offered him to God. After that both the father and mother walked around the room and thanked each person who had helped keep their baby alive as long as possible.

Though this happened some time ago, the pastoral experience it fostered continues to touch me, and no doubt everyone who was present that day. It illuminated a simple truth – we need one another. We need one another in our mourning, our problem solving, our fears, our faith journeys. It doesn't matter how gifted, wealthy, or powerful we are. We simply can't go it alone. None of these qualities keep us from getting sick or from losing our homes in wildfires or tornados. None of these qualities guarantees we won't lose our job, our life savings, or our child. That day has served as a reminder that each of us is called to be a loving community—not sentimental naïve love but a practical, unpolished kind that shows up, listens and tells the truth.

Today, after years of ministry, listening to patients, friends and loved ones has taught me a great deal about the power of loss and the potential for enriched healing. Our life journeys consist of turning points and passages. These passages become our personal stories of faith and hope. They are the tests and trials that shape us. Each of the foundational influences I've described has impacted my desire to offer a welcoming, faith-filled presence to individuals, families, and communities seeking healing and reconciliation. I look forward to sharing these gifts for as long as I am able.

Finally, in the Judeo-Christian tradition, the word for peace is shalom. We experience shalom as an act of God's graciousness in our lives. Such peace is more than simply an absence of conflict. Shalom really means wholeness. It plays a vital role in building and protecting the well-being of all our communities including our families, our neighborhoods, and our workplaces.

Who Shall We Be?

To greet someone with "Shalom" is to ask, "How is it with you? Do you have work? Does your family have enough food? "Do you have adequate shelter?" It implies that the one who asks the question accepts some level of responsibility for the other person's well-being. We offer this gift of shalom to another in many ways – by listening and affirming and by our acts of goodwill.

Shalom points to the idea of being well. Similarly, the terms "cure" and "Healing" reflect two distinct avenues to the same end: becoming well. Used in this context, "cure" refers primarily to specific acts of scientific intervention. These interventions could consist of surgery, the taking of prescription drugs, and the application of technology. "Healing," on the other hand, points to a set of possibilities that everyone, especially health care professionals, can bring to a seemingly incurable situation. While a healing approach may not always change a medical outcome, or control social or environmental problems, it can positively affect our own and other's health. A healing approach encompasses assets that all of us—physicians, nurses, family, friends, and colleagues – already possess. When we choose to offer these assets to others, we foster their feelings of safety, wholeness, and hope. Sharing these assets also tends to create in us a sense of belonging and of being connected to one another.

If cure cannot be separated from healing, neither can healing be disconnected from shalom. Each of us contributes immeasurably to this totality called health by promoting the following aspects of peace and healing: hospitality, presence, listening, compassion, advocacy, acceptance, hope, and gratitude.

Consider this

The doctor who shared the three chaplain directives in this story demonstrated the same values in his medical practice. He also expected this from his physician colleagues and caregivers. I remember a particular meeting with him, when several participants began to argue about an event that had taken place in the Critical Care unit. Though the confrontation focused on some aspect of protocol, not patient treatment, the conversation escalated. Finally, the doctor who organized the meeting said simply: "You cannot listen unless and until you stop talking."

Imagine how much our world might heal if we consistently practiced these skills.

Who Shall We Be?

Imagine what I would have missed if I had slipped out of the hospital and gone home to bed instead of visiting a dying eight-year-old boy who asked to say a prayer for me.

Imagine the consequences of not listening carefully to a troubled friend or a family who just lost a beloved grandparent.

Think of a situation that prompted you to offer solutions instead of simply listening. Telling the truth could be as straight forward as telling a gravely ill or troubled friend that you love her or him.

Think of a time when you have "shown up" though you might have preferred to stay away. In my experience, showing up has typically provided lessons and opportunities to grow in grace and goodness.

Each of these experiences offers a rich opportunity to explore values that enhance our ministries, our professional practices, our friendships, and the quality of our lives.

Wisdom Wellness - An idea that has come alive

Several years ago, Minneapolis clinical nurse specialist Judy Peters concluded that empowering seniors to live independently in their homes made sense.

Who Shall We Be?

"It's simple for me," she explained. "I am wired to be who I am by all the people and experiences that have shaped my belief system. Everything from my personal beginnings to my life work in health care has shaped who I am as a person and as a nurse. It also has shaped how I see care giving and helping others maintain their health and independence."

This is how Wisdom Wellness was created. This belief system includes a piece of wisdom from Rev. Doctor Martin Luther King, Junior," she added: *"Life's most urgent question: What are you doing for others? 'I believe we are called to give what we can, when we can, to those who need what we have."*

Judy's idea to create Wisdom Wellness emerged in 2016 and continues to evolve. The goal is to leverage community resources, existing health insurance, and supportive community partnerships to produce a unique aging at home service for seniors. Her efforts enable seniors to remain happy, healthy, and safe at home, where their wishes, voices, and cultural connections are respected and protected.

This enterprising plan includes social and functional caring provided by interdisciplinary and intergenerational professional volunteers. These fully trained professionals combine their clinical wisdom with new perspectives on aging. The new perspectives deliver a rich and energy-filled experience for their elderly patients and families.

"Growing up I was raised by a single mom, living on food stamps and early versions of the welfare system," Judy explained. "I also received unconditional love from my grandparents who were immigrants from the Acores. The food we ate, the language we spoke, the faith we practiced, and the ways of everyday life at home were firmly grounded in the Azorean way. It's a culture that focuses on family and faith. This included respecting and valuing our grandparents, aunts, uncles, and blood relatives."

So, who are these Wisdom Wellness volunteers? "They consist of a dedicated group of individuals with a diverse range of clinical and non-clinical skills," explained Judy. "They also bring with them a community understanding, and a deep collective commitment to social caring."

All the volunteers embrace a desire to make a measurable difference in the lives of those in need. By integrating their broad range of experience with their richly empathetic approach to care, they strive to create a positive impact on both individual lives and on the broader community in which they live. By sharing their time, talent, and resources, these volunteers also experience a genuine sense of purpose as individuals and professionals.

"In my health care-based experience, every aspect of caring or being cared for begins with a skill that Wisdom

Who Shall We Be?

Wellness calls a *listening heart*," Judy explained. "Caring for our own aging family members has taught us a great deal about the complexities in navigating America's traditional health care system. Our aging elders living with chronic care needs, such as hearing, vision, and cognitive losses, create challenges for the entire family. We often felt lost and struggled with how to manage these conditions in between care visits. The Wisdom Wellness program is designed to addresses such challenging health conditions typically associated with aging."

Judy is often asked, why do you do the work you do, especially when you are not even paid to do it? "It's simple for me," she says. "I am wired to be who I am by all the people and experiences I've received along the way. Each of these has shaped my belief system. For me, growing up didn't mean making money. It meant being present and tending to what needed to be done for your family and neighbors."

Her grandparents believed that everyone deserved a chance to do better, and that's what this country meant to them. "They frequently sponsored people coming to the United States from the Azores," Judy explained. "This meant they co-signed rental units, and helped the newcomers find jobs in factories, construction, bakeries, and house cleaning." Her grandparents then helped the new immigrant neighbors get settled by giving them their personal pots, pans, dishes, and even clothing. This included everything from blankets, and mattresses, to towels, and more. The gestures were offered as welcoming gifts to help newly arrived families get started in America," said Judy.

"I learned very early that love and doing good are part of what makes the world and each of us better. My grandmother was my superhero. Even though there were only four of us living in her house, she cooked huge pots of food, baked countless loaves of bread, and malasadas (fried dough dipped in sugar). She sewed dozens of shirts, dresses, pants, curtains, tablecloths, and pillowcases, all for new arrivals to this country. Some of my favorite adventures with my grandparents included driving around looking for items on the side of the road that could be repurposed for our new immigrant friends and family.

The following Wisdom Wellness values have been influenced by Judy's immigrant family. They also provide a foundation that supports the most tender yet complex issues that surface during the aging process.

We value each person's lived story

We believe people are not their illness, disease, or life challenge.

We work with the person who is self-care managing his or her chronic, complex conditions, and we are led by their voice and by what matters most to them.

We use our hearts and problem-solving abilities to bring a respectful and supportive experience to each encounter with the population we serve.

We believe in listening to understand and not rush to "fix." Instead, we walk with and alongside the seniors in their self-care management work.

We offer help, encouragement, and support.

We are good stewards of our resources.

We cherish our relationship- based connections with those we serve, and those who give of their time and talents to this important work.

When Wisdom Wellness immerged in 2016, Judy and her colleagues faced another big question: Could they provide clinical support services to seniors living in a low-income housing? It appeared that most residents in these facilities had insurance, though many struggled to understand their benefit coverage or how best to access existing community resources. Then, in 2017, together with other volunteer nurses, the team created a pathway to service by offering blood pressure checks and by answering general health questions expressed by the residents. This service took place two hours per week in the community library of a designated low-income apartment building.

The approach found success among the community residents. The volunteers were able to build trust within the community and good relationships with its members. The program grew. Hours increased, care services expanded, and nurse practitioners joined the team of volunteers. Their work now reached beyond health education, care coordination, and advocacy. It also added just in time care, plus triaging clinical needs. Other services included a medication reconciliation program with pharmacy direct monthly delivery to the residents. In June 2024, Wisdom Wellness became incorporated as a Minnesota nonprofit. The program now provides weekly reminders on medication and treatment plans to support a comprehensive elders self-care management success at home.

Who receives care from Wisdom Wellness today and who will receive these services going forward? "Today Wisdom Wellness serves older adults living in low-income senior housing," said Judy. "Care is provided by the combined expertise of volunteer nurse practitioners, registered nurses, and community health workers. This care takes place once a week in an on-site space located in a low-income, independent, residential living community. Volunteers address each elder's existing and emerging health challenges at no cost. All services, support, and assistances fall within the volunteer's scope of practice. Also, volunteers follow the elders' individual treatment plan from their healthcare providers. All aspects of care coincide with best practices and protocols, as well as supervision from an on-site clinical practice leader.

Wisdom Wellness work is not restricted by the number of assigned visits determined by a benefits provider or diagnosis. Instead, the services are determined by the senior's voice and by what that individual believes he or she needs. This approach creates the necessary time and space for whole-person centered, relationship-based care. The normal aging processes often finds older adults in need of more time and accommodations. This likely includes thoughtful, repetitive explanations of the self-care process. It also includes medication management within the elder's daily life routine.

Social and functional caring define the heart of Wisdom Wellness. Listening hearts offered by all the volunteers play a vital role in the well-being of each person served by the organization. This is especially true among those seniors who live alone and could be isolated. Friendly conversation, shared activities, and opportunities to revisit the same topics weekly with Wisdom Wellness volunteers can brighten a senior's day. It also improves overall moods and creates opportunities for staff to identify any declines in overall health.

"This is about getting to know an elder's lived story, by offering unlimited one on one attention that is not defined by a time constraint," adds Judy. "This relationship creates a better opportunity for correct diagnoses. It also fosters trust and respect. It's an environment in which the senior feels valued and understood." Health education and health promotion programs further enhance the value of these relationships by providing monthly talk circles or Lunch and Learn.

In addition to social and functional caring, Wisdom Wellness offers medication pick-up service. This ensures that seniors enrolled in the pharmacy pick up service receive their medication promptly and safely. Wisdom Wellness volunteers involved with the medication reconciliation program also help individuals who need to access the medication. Each of these services contributes to their overall wellbeing and peace of mind. "The program enables us to assure that a self-care managing senior has access to all the medication resources necessary to support his or her treatment plans, as prescribed by their physician," Judy added.

These kinds of services enable Wisdom Wellness to create a valuable space for synergy across different generations and professional backgrounds. By combining the clinical wisdom of current and retired professionals, with new perspectives and energy of emerging professionals and students, Wisdom Wellness can offer a rich environment based on shared community support.

Who Shall We Be?

"Our country's current health care system is exceptional for acute or emergency health issues, a planned event, and a controlled procedure," Judy added. "When people have multiple chronic conditions and are living with the complexities of social determinants of health, their true needs and solutions cannot be codified or completed in a time limiting number of visits. Nothing brought this reality to me more than when I worked in senior living or congregated community dwelling spaces for older adults." What she discovered was: When people can afford to have help with:

Setting up medications and reminders to take medications

Setting up doctor appointments

Changing bandages

Figuring out insurance coverage

Advocating for their health needs

Periodic checks of their blood pressure and blood sugar

Grocery shopping and meal planning

And organized socialization, they do much better cognitively, physically, and functionally than those who cannot afford this kind of support.

"These, plus some friendly drop in visits helped improve individual's cognitively, physically and functionally far more than those who do not receive these supports," Judy explained.

"After my hospital nursing experience, I knew the hospital was not the place for me, I needed an environment in which I could practice with people and families because I believed that health care and caregiving are not episodic events. They are relational."

She has spent more than four decades immersed in clinical nursing in numerous settings. These include for profit and non-profit organizations, traditional systems, and start-ups working to develop innovative new care models, technologies and new ways of delivering health care.

"At the end of all these experiences, my conclusion was always the same," she said: opportunities to work with great people who entered the helping profession to provide care and support that they would want their own family members to receive. All wanting to do better. Yet, all challenged by the limits of health systems, specifically the limited amount of time spent with patients, and the lack of coverage that limited continuing services. These challenges found families trying to decide between care services, medication refills, food, rent, and more," Judy witnessed.

"It turns out that I did learn a lot. Being a public health nurse and a seasoned care coordinator, plus a family care giver taught me a skill set, as well as frustration and a passion to offer something different to people who don't have people to help. It confirmed for me that a new version of independency as people aged was possible. It just did not fit into model of one or two time visits every 30 to 90 days. It also taught me that, if you tack on limited or unstable family supports, low income, unstable housing, and historical trauma from systems intended to help, it likely results in physical and mental health decline. This tends to produce overuse of the emergency room, depression, multiple inpatient rebounding, and an array of everyday social and functional areas of decline.

    I knew there were health care professionals looking for a next chapter in which they could share their time and talents. I also believed, if they heard the story of what I was trying to do through Wisdom Wellness, they would see a space for their heart and skills. Tapping these colleagues with diverse clinical and non-clinical professional backgrounds, and a deep commitment to social caring would assure a pipeline of helping hearts and hands to sustain Wisdom Wellness."

Hooray for Homeys

My daughter and I have always enjoyed visiting the Chautauqua Institution. The not-for-profit, 75-acre educational center sits at the edge of a charming lake in southwestern New York State. While it is a perfect setting for a summer get-away, it also offers an educational experience dedicated to exploring the best in human values. Additionally, Chautauqua presentations examine important religious, social and political issues of our times. Each topic and speaker encouraged thoughtful involvement and discussion from guests and their families. This is exactly what my daughter and I discovered during our recent trip to Chautauqua: The topic for the week featured rehabilitation of our country's most prolific and dangerous gang members.

Father Greg Boyle, a native Angeleno and Jesuit priest, served as our chaplain that week. Previously Father Boyle served as pastor of Dolores Mission Church in Boyle Heights, California. During the period, from 1986 to 1992, Dolores Mission was considered the poorest Catholic parish in Los Angeles. The area also faced the highest concentration of gang activity in the city. Father Greg's parish encompassed Aliso Village and Pico Gardens, then the largest public housing projects west of the Mississippi. It also served as home for the highest concentration of gang activity. This unfortunate achievement took place when, Los Angeles had already gained a reputation as the gang capital of the world.

Here, during the so-called decade of death is where Father Boyle witnessed the devastating impact of gang violence on his community. It began in the late 1980s and peaked at the point of 1,000 gang-related killings in 1992. This took place at a time when law enforcement tactics and criminal justice policies of suppression and mass incarceration served as the primary means to end gang violence. However, where others only saw criminals, Father Greg saw people in need of help. He soundly rejected the idea that it is God's plan that anyone should die of a gang member's bullet. "There is no us and them, he explained, just us."

In 1988, Father Greg, or G, as his homeys now call him, started what would become Homeboy Industries, the largest gang rehabilitation and re-entry program in the world. For thirty years, this organization has served as a beacon of hope in Los Angeles for formerly gang-involved and previously incarcerated individuals who seek to change their life paths. Within the Homeboy Industries community, people find their lives getting redefined by love. It is an organization that employs and trains former gang members through a range of social enterprises. Homeboy Industries further, provides critical services including mental health, job training, drug rehabilitation and much more. These services plus the experience of belonging to a supportive community are offered to thousands of men and women who walk through the doors every year seeking a better life.

"We work with a population that nobody desires to work with," explains Father Greg. "Each year we welcome thousands of people through our doors seeking to transform their lives. Whether joining our eighteen- month employment and re-entry program or seeking discrete services such as tattoo removal or substance abuse resources, our clients are embraced by a community of kinship and offered a variety of free wraparound services to facilitate their healing and growth. In addition to serving almost 7000 members of the immediate Los Angeles community in 2018, our flagship 18-month employment and re-entry program was offered to over 400 men and women."

Father Greg's message of hope, redemption, and the inherent worth of every individual transcends cultural and ideological boundaries by inspiring people from all walks of life to come together in community to help those who live on the margins of our society," explained Thomas Vozzo, Chief Executive Officer of Homeboy Industries.

All this history would set the table for Father Boyle's presentations during our week at Chautauqua. And he did not come alone. He brought four rehabilitated gang members with him. Four homeys who would educate the rest of us in what it means to belong to a gang, and how they each navigated his way to freedom with the assistance of Homeboy Industries.

As someone who grew up in a small Wisconsin town, I knew nothing about gangs or their members. My knowledge of gang activity was confined to the two bullies who stole my lunch money while I was walking to school. I don't recall ever feeling unsafe or frightened of my neighbors. My family created a secure space for my brother and me, as well as for our children to grow and participate in the world around us.

And now my daughter and I were about to discover the meaning of homeboy or homey. We also would learn about the brutal and destructive world from which they had come. Then we learned about the unspeakable cruelty and physical abuse these young men endured as children. We tried to understand the constant fighting among gang members, the common gunshot injuries and deaths, and the drug use and drug sales among gang members.

After that, each homey described how he had participated in a Homeboy drug recovery program. They described services that included everything from mental health to job training, anger management, community building, tattoo removal, breaking free from gang violence and cycles of poverty and incarceration.

Today, Homeboy Industries is the largest gang intervention, rehabilitation and re-entry program in the world. Father Greg, with parish and community members, had adopted what was viewed as a radical approach to dealing with gang members: treat them as human beings. The results have been remarkable.

For example," I was at a point in which I wanted to give up because I felt stuck," explained Norma Lopez. My record was keeping me from finding a job. I had nothing on my resume. Prospective employers wanted to hire me though when they found out I had a record and felonies, they denied my application.

Who Shall We Be?

I couldn't find a job anywhere. That's when someone told me to come to Homeboy.

Donna, our Director of Legal services helped me bring my felonies down to misdemeanors and expunge my record. I have so many things on my resume now! It feels really, really good. I've been sobor for almost six years. I don't feel stuck today. I feel that I'm able to move forward. No matter what's going on in my life I know I can get through it.

It just gives me a lot of peace and hope that no matter what I'm going through, I don't have to be alone today. I have people who are there for me and help me, even if it's just a hug or an "I'm here for you." I've never had this much support.

Life shows up. I used to run when life showed up. I don't have to run today. I have people who are there for me, with me, to go through it."

This grace filled thank you for goodness and healing came from Norma Lopez, a woman who, at a most critical intersection in her life, found her way to Homeboy industries. She is far from alone.

"We work with a population that nobody desires to work with" explains Father Greg. "Each year we welcome thousands of people through our doors seeking to transform their lives. Whether joining our eighteen- month employment and re-entry program or seeking discrete services such as tattoo removal or substance abuse resources, our clients are embraced by a community of kinship and offered a variety of free wraparound services to facilitate their healing and growth. In addition to serving almost 7000 members of the immediate Los Angeles community in 2018, our flagship 18-month employment and re-entry program was offered to over 400 men and women.

History has shown that the homeys come to the program not only for the services, but for the spirit and values that Father Greg has infused into what is a technically designated secular nonprofit. While Father Greg still believes employment is important, as evidenced by the hundreds of former gang members and recently incarcerated people who work in Homeboy's bakery, recycling program, and solar energy project, Father Greg has come to a deeper truth: personal transformation requires healing the scars that prevent people from realizing their unshakeable goodness, their nobility in God's eyes. He believes in restorative justice – reconnecting people with their wholeness.

In 2024 Father Boyle received the Presidential Medal of Freedom from President Joseph R. Biden, Jr. The Presidential Medal of Freedom is the United States' highest civilian honor. "This recognition honors the many thousands of men and women who have walked through our doors at Homeboy Industries. It acknowledges their dignity, their nobility and the courage of their tenderness. It also underscores for us the invitation to no longer punish a wound, but to seek its healing.

Father Greg's ministry through Homeboy industries exemplifies the transformative power of compassion, forgiveness, and second chances. His unwavering dedication to building bridges across divides and promote understanding through compassion, kinship and tenderness underscores the importance of empathy and connection in creating a more harmonious society. Each person who chooses to begin this transformative journey brings his or her unique experiences, wishes and goals. For example, George Nunez began his transformative journey at Homeboy as a trainee. He then embraced every opportunity and took full advantage of the classes offered. He also leaned on the guidance of case managers, who helped him become vulnerable enough to embrace change. He attributes much of his growth to the unwavering support of Father Boyle, who gave him a chance to renew his life also believed in him when he needed it most. Reflecting on his journey, George acknowledges that, while he might not be where he wants to be yet, he's far from where he used to be. "Homeboy Industries gave me a place and a face," he explained. "A place to call home and a face, meaning I no longer feel the need to have a mask or a brick wall up. I can be vulnerable and accepting of the real me." George has been honored to share his story.

Founded in 1988 as jobs for the Future in 1988, Father Greg's relentless commitment to standing with the most marginalized individuals has led to Homeboy Industries to becoming the largest rehabilitation program in the world for formerly incarcerated, gang involved people. Homeboys healing centric program serves nearly 10,000 people in Los Angeles annually while acting as a global model for hundreds of organizations in the U.S. and around the world who have been inspired by Father Greg's work as part of the Global homeboy network. In 2020, Homeboy Industries received the Conrad N. Hilton Humanitarian Prize, for its extraordinary contributions toward alleviating human suffering.

"Father Greg's message of hope, redemption, and the inherent worth of every individual transcends cultural and ideological boundaries. It inspires people from all walks of life to come together in community, whether it is to heal as a community or simply grow in goodness, we need one another," explained Thomas Vozzo, Chief Executive Officer of Homeboy Industries.

My daughter and I learned a great deal about the life of gangs and gang members during our week at Chautauqua. We also were moved by Father Greg's message of hope, redemption, and the inherent value of every individual. No matter where we are on our own life journeys, this felt like a gift that transcends all cultural and ideological boundaries. It inspires people from all walks of life to come together in community. Whether it is to heal as community or simply grow in goodness, we need one another.

By weeks end my daughter and I had learned a great deal about the life of gangs and the implications for those who join them. One can only imagine that the four homeys who met us and shared their shocking, though healing stories, also provided one more step in their journey toward wholeness. I say that because of the heartfelt response it prompted from their audience. It was a response that inspired virtually everyone to jump from their seats and rush forward to embrace each of the homeys. I too was delighted to embrace a guy who had gone through a process of having more than 100 tattoos removed. He explained to those of us who knew little about tattoo removal that he did not wish to share his previous gang affiliation with any interested gang members.

All of this prompted me to think about my 40 years serving as a chaplain. One of the first lessons I learned taught me about the priceless value and purpose of telling one's story. Whether it's a patient processing a life-ending cancer diagnosis, or a gang member wrestling with stumbling blocks that prevent his or her recovery, their story matters. In my experience it is exceedingly difficult to know where we are going unless we know where have been.

This homey also prompted me to think about our country and the world around us. Why do we struggle so to resolve the problems of polarization, greed, power, and violence. If we can't listen to one another's needs, or disagree with their color, culture, or goals, how can we hope to heal.

Father Boyle is the author of the 2010 *New York Times*-bestseller *Tattoos on the Heart: The Power of Boundless Compassion*. His book, *Barking to the Choir: The Power of Radical Kinship*, was published in 2017.

He has received the California Peace Prize and been inducted into the California Hall of Fame. In 2014, President Obama named Father Boyle a *Champion of Change*. He received the University of Notre Dame's 2017 Laetare Medal, the oldest honor given to American Catholics. Currently, he serves as a committee member of California Governor Gavin Newsom's Economic and Job Recovery Task Force as a response to COVID-19

My Wise Friend Iris

I once enjoyed a friendship with a wonderful women named Iris. Iris was in her 80s and recently widowed when we met. Her husband had been an Episcopal priest for many years, and the two of them enjoyed their work within our faith community.

One day shortly after my ordination to the diaconate, I asked Iris how she felt about women in ministry. It was a time when a great deal of emotion whirled around an event called the Philadelphia Eleven. This occasion consisted of the ordination to priesthood of eleven women. It also took place before the

Episcopal church had authorized such an ordination. Coincidentally, it occurred when I faced my own ordination to the diaconate, a separate ordained ministry within the church. Unlike priesthood, the diaconate is described as a servant ministry, which influenced my choice to become a chaplain.

However, to my surprise, this event also prompted a good deal of anger and loss of friendships within my original faith community. Arguments ensued about the validity of women serving in an ordained capacity. A member of my prayer group simply stopped speaking to me. I ultimately moved to a more hospitable diocese. That is when I met Iris.

I eventually shared this story with her and asked what she thought about it. She responded with her usual humor and clarity plus her opinion about how our country and even some of its churches worshipped too many gods— including money, power, control, misogyny, racism and more. For her the problem was not the ordination of women but a problem with values. Then she turned to me and added, "For all the colleagues and friends who have asked me, "Where is God's light hiding in this treatment of women who have made a commitment to ministry, let me tell you a story." I sat down and listened carefully to every word.

Long ago, one deep, dark night, a small party of powerful gods met to discuss a frightening revelation – a threat of such scale that it endangered their very survival as gods. It seemed

Who Shall We Be?

that, while they had been reclining upon their ample backsides, boasting of their admirable achievements, a rumor began circulating among the mortals. The rumor claimed that they, mere mortals, also held the potential for divinity. Deeply disturbed at this career-threatening breakthrough, the gods made haste to convene a blue-ribbon task force to study the matter. The impressive guest list said it all. Fertility gods, war gods, sports gods, celebrity gods – the works – every majestic mover and supreme shaker whose reputation stood to suffer from this looming disaster received a summons.

The meeting day arrived, and delegates of every celestial order appeared. First came registration and refreshments... a bit of small talk. Quickly, however, the standard schmoozing gave way to a clamorous cacophony framed by one burning question: 'What are we going to do about these ungrateful boors who call themselves mortals?"

"Who do they think they are?" snorted an irritable investment god. "For years I've heard nothing but whine, whine, whine Buy this. 'Sell that. Maybe mutual funds. No, make that wheat futures. I can't remember when they haven't been making some kind of demand. Now it looks as if they want to compete with us, for heaven's sake. They might be tiresome to work with, but if mortals ever do find this divine spark, I would be out of business. We all could be standing in the royal unemployment lines!"

"You're right! Roared a defense god. "A discovery like this could spell supremely slashed budgets and heavenly hiring freezes. Why, imagine what would happen if they figured out how to get along without us… or with each other, God forbid! You know the old chestnut, 'no bombs, no budgets.' That means downsized operations. Maybe even early retirements. If this spark gets out of the bag, we can say good-bye golf games and hello quality improvement consultants.

"No doubt about it, we need to settle down and figure out where on earth we can hide the spark of divinity so that mortals never get their hands on it."

Ideas whirled about the conference hall – wild and complicated schemes. Gods whose social paths rarely crossed now huddled together, oddly linked through a common fear for their future security. What a throng of stewing sovereigns they made.

Unfortunately, their rank outshone their cleverness, for none came up with a solution that the others could agree upon.

"Upstarts," grumbled a football deity. "They have no idea just how tricky this god business can be when it lands in the wrong hands. "

Who Shall We Be?

Everyone nodded, appreciative of his discerning insight, The day passed with no sign of a solution. Twilight seeped across the frozen landscape. Currents of life retired to their silent roots, waiting for winter and some solution to the immediate crisis. The god's mused. Beleaguered delegates reconvened, pinched-faced and pale, to tick off a lackluster list of ideas.

"How about hiding this spark of divinity in an oyster at the bottom of the sea?" offered one. "Or perhaps in a distant galaxy?

"No, no, no, growled an IRS god. "Why, in no time, some diver or astronaut will discover it and steal it away."

"How about inside a smoldering volcano"" proposed another. "Or in an eagle's nest high upon a mountain peak?" advised a third. " Perhaps, among the bunchberries that cover the forest floor?"

Disapproving murmurs followed each suggestion. At last, they gave up and prepared to leave. Suddenly an elderly woman, a Hearth keeper, raised her hand tentatively to report that she might have the answer to the question of where to hide the diving spark. '" What is it? demanded the chief executive god, who, by this time had a migraine and wanted to go home. "Speak up madam."

The hearth keeper rose to her feet with a certain grace and rather floated to the front of the conference hall. Far less flamboyant than the other delegates, she wore a simple woolen tunic with a linen shawl about her shoulders. With her silver hair secured in an amber clasp, she exuded both mystery and wisdom. She was known throughout the countryside not for theatrical, godlike acts but for her capacity to listen. Most of the other gods found her slightly strange, as she always seemed preoccupied with the well-being of humans. Though none of the gods had ever actually caught her speaking to a mortal, some suspected her of giving away trade secrets.

The woman whispered her proposal to the chief executive god. He brightened. Normally he might have dismissed a Hearth keeper's idea, but he had nothing better to offer – and besides, he could hardly keep from admiring her cleverness.

He shared her idea with his assistant, who laughed out loud with delight. The gloom lifted slightly from the room as one by one, the guests passed the Hearth keeper's suggestion among themselves. Nonetheless, even in their excitement, they spoke in a whisper for fear that some gate-crashing mortal might overhear.

"It's perfect," crowed the defense god jubilantly. "Why even heat-seeking missiles couldn't find it there. No one will find the spark of divinity now. We need never again contend with those brazen humans overstepping their authority." With that, the

Who Shall We Be?

delegates voted unanimously in favor of the Hearth keeper's idea and then departed from the convention.

A year later, in the month of December, two men plodded along a dark and lonely road in the northern territory. They walked without words, staring sadly at the night sky. Snow drifted about their feet in soft meringue peaks. Disillusioned and brokenhearted, they leaned into the wind. The winter landscape lay unadorned except by a frozen sky. They heard no music beyond the bitter wind. The night bore them only icy tears. They had been searching for a divine spark, but tonight they abandoned hope. Now the men simply longed for home a warm fire.

An elderly woman stood alone at the roadside. Bundled in a simple woolen tunic, she watched from beneath her shawl The travelers moved slowly, driving themselves onward with thoughts of a warm hearth. When they came within hearing distance, she called to them pleasantly: "Who are you, and what brings you out on such a night as this?"

"We're we are mortals," called back the younger man through the darkness. "We've been searching. We have combed the valleys and hillsides, convinced that we would find a divine spark, a light of implication."

"But why do you seek such a light?" queried the woman.

"Because we have become impoverished by our affluence and broken by our own powerlessness," lamented the older man. "We hunger for hope and yearn for reconciliation. We are overturned by tension and confused by the world's empty promises. We need such a light to show us the way."

The woman inquired further, "What makes you think this divine spark exists? And tell me, too, what would you do with it should you find it?"

The older man continued his bitter repining, as if he hadn't heard her. "Snow falls now on our path. We have watched the skies for signs. We have wandered the roads of our past questioning what we might have done differently to lead us to this wondrous spark. We have traveled through streets of violence and oppression in hope of kindling a new flame in our hearts. We envisioned healing and peace."

The woman reached out to receive their sorrow and pressed it to her heart. Then she asked if they would accompany her to her hearth. The exhausted and freezing men agreed, and the three set off together into the night of discovery.

"Do you know that night is the birth of all things?" The woman asked her two companions. "Night wears a mantle of snow; shivering in the darkness, it watches and waits. Winter is a waiting season and a time of breakthroughs."

Who Shall We Be?

The men listened but did not understand. They walked in silence until they came to the woman's hut. She invited them into warm by her fire and refresh themselves.

"Break bread with me," she implored. "Let your strength return before you continue your search."

Inside the hut encircled by warmth, the travelers accepted a bit of cheese and hot tea from the woman while they dried their clothes near her hearth. Her simple cottage boosted their spirits, a cozy respite from their heavy burdens and paralyzing cold.

Meanwhile, the woman busied herself preparing a parcel of food, which she wrapped in her linen shawl. She helped the men into their coats and wished them well as they set out for home.

"This should see you through the night." she said handing them the small bundle. "Blessings on you and yours," she called warmly behind them as they disappeared into the dark.

Near dawn, the men came to a small village. Exhausted from fighting the wind and snow, they took shelter in a barn. They settled themselves into a mound of straw and thought about the strange woman. They thought also about their failed search for the spark of divinity.

"We have not accomplished anything that we set out to do." The older man sighed. "All the good intentions. All the dreams and plans. All our hopes for success have failed. It just doesn't seem fair."

In thoughtful stillness, they contemplated the events of the past months. At last, the younger man pulled the woman's bundle from beneath his coat to see what she had given them to eat. He laid the contents upon the straw to share with his friend: a piece of cheese, a loaf of bread, some dried apples, and a few hazelnuts. Beneath the food lay an envelope secured by an amber clasp, the kind a woman would wear to secure her log hair.

They ate, while the older man removed the amber clasp and opened the envelope. He examined the contents carefully. On a single piece of parchment was written the following:

Break this bread and think of me
A sage who has lived enough to see
That peace and fairness and love are real
For those who hear and forgive and feel
Who keep the hearth and tend the meal
Who warm a space for others to heal
Who nurture a child and care for the sick
And seek to be just is all that they pick
Who lighten the dark that others might see
And think with their heart and learn just to be
Who know how to laugh and know how to grieve

Who Shall We Be?

And celebrate life, both its pain and reprieve.

For you who have searched every place far and near

You but need to know that there's nothing to fear

For all that is well will be well from now on

With you who have wandered and struggled anon

For low as you looked everywhere for the spark

The light that you seek lives right in your heart

Heavenly Whole Wheat Bread

Perhaps nothing enhances the quality of our lives more than preparing and eating good food. And nothing offers a richer example of shared life than bread. Whether we speak of bread in terms of food, money, community, or comfort, it enjoys an expansive history of association with nurturing and healing.

2 cups lukewarm milk

2 packets active dry yeast

1/3 cup honey

3 cups whole wheat flour

1 egg beaten

2 teaspoons salt

½ teaspoon nutmeg

½ cup butter

3-4 cups unbleached all-purpose flour

Pour milk into mixing bowl. Stir in 1 teaspoon honey; add yeast and whole wheat flour and cover loosely. Leave for 20 minutes. Mix in the rest of the honey, the egg, salt, nutmeg, butter and 3 to 3 ½ cups of the all purpose flour. Mix until dough begins to pull away from sides of the bowl. Place the dough on a board and knead for 8 to 10 minutes, until smooth and elastic. Divide into two shaped loaves, and place in two greased bread pans. Let rise until doubled in bulk, about 1 to 1 ½ hours. Bake in

Who Shall We Be?

preheated 350-degree oven for 35 to 40 minutes. Share one loaf with a friend.

Healing Born of Gratitude

My mother died in late July. I remember it as the season when fireweed and Queen Anne's lace bloomed along the roadsides near our Wisconsin home. Mom loved wildflowers and birds. The two of us spent many hours wandering through pastures and along Lowes Creek identifying both.

Mom's death signaled the end of a chapter for my brother and me. Our father had already passed, and the home that defined our childhood now stood empty, as we faced sorting out the personal effects and financial affairs left behind.

Who Shall We Be?

Though we all experience the loss of beloved family members, the passing of parents touches each of us in different ways. For example, Mom grew up under challenging circumstances. Her young life began when her parents left her in an orphanage, so that they might pursue their traveling music entertainment business. Though Mom was just an infant at the time, an aunt and uncle eventually adopted her. They provided her with a good home, and a fine education, yet she described growing up as a lonely journey.

That would change. Eventually, the loss of her parents, plus the death of her first-born child might have left her empty, and disheartened. Instead, she grew into a gentle, faith-filled, welcoming, woman, who loved to cook and care for others. And everyone loved her food and thoughtful hospitality.

My first experience watching Mom work her generous magic, with a complete stranger, took place when she told me that an elderly man with racehorses had moved in next door. I quickly called my friend Robin with this exciting news. The only thing more exciting than dressing up our own horses and galloping through the woods was the prospect of meeting someone who raced horses.

"Horse crazy," our parents called us. No piano lessons, no summer camp, no party dresses for us. Robin and I thought of nothing but horses and all the adventures we could cook up with our horses. In fact, I had already decided to become a jockey, so this would fit right into my training program. But first, I jumped into my new Tony Lama boots, strapped on a favorite Gene Autry belt and trotted over to meet the new neighbor.

The sagging barn was a little disappointing. Daylight streamed through the unpainted boards. Pink hollyhocks poked between an empty corncrib and a crumbling cement silo. Holes near the barn's foundation hinted of rats—or worse. It certainly didn't look like Churchill Downs, but maybe he had a property-improvement plan. Suddenly, a voice shot out, "Get the hell off my property!" I wasted no time doing just that.

This was not going to be easy, but after discussing a plan with Robin, we decided to try a different approach. The next day, I waited until late in the afternoon, when the old man left the barn and headed for home. Once his car rattled out the driveway, I slipped across the pasture and into the tumbledown building. Armed with my Labrador retriever, Sam, I crept into a small feed room that smelled of molasses and alfalfa. Two horses peered curiously from their comfy box stalls. The place looked modest but tidy. A grooming box next to the stalls held brushes, hoof picks and sweat scrapers. A stack of clean towels, buckets, saddle soap, and assorted veterinary products neatly lined the shelves. But harnesses, not saddles, hung on the wall. A picture on the wall read "Dan Patch" beneath it.

Who Shall We Be?

I didn't stay long but vowed to come back to spy on the activities and then report all the details to Robin. So, the next day, armed with my mother's birding binoculars, I stole through the trees and ducked under some small jack pines near the edge of his exercise track. Much to my surprise, I learned that he owned harness racing horses, not saddle horses – two fine looking geldings—one a trotter and one a pacer. He worked each horse every day while I spied from a safe distance.

Eventually, he discovered me and bellowed that I had better beat it. Now! I hightailed it for home, but already had decided that Robin and I were going to wear the guy down. An old horseman, with his deeply lined face and powerful hands that held the reins almost daintily, was not going to get away from us. After watching this training routine for a couple of weeks, I worked up the courage to try something new. This time, I saddled up my horse Koko and rode over to his place. Hopefully he couldn't reach me with those huge hands, if I stayed on the horse.

Koko and I watched and waited as he led the pacer up the drive in my direction. To my surprise, he just walked around us without a word. At the edge of the track, he adjusted the hobbles, checked the horse's blinkers, and climbed into the sulky. It was as if he didn't even see us standing on the path. Koko and I just eyed him silently as he led the horse onto the track.

Watching the workout made my heart pound. I had no idea pacers moved at such speed. Dust swirled beneath the sulky wheels, and I could hear the harness slap against the horse's flanks. After completing the exercise session, Mr. Stall walked his winded horse twice around the track to cool him out. He then headed toward the driveway where Koko and I waited nervously.

What's yer name? he grunted, climbing out of the sulky and releasing the harness overcheck.

"Mary," I replied, attempting to calm the tremble in my voice.

"Okay Marian, if you're so blessed interested in what I do around here, climb off that old nag and cool this one out."

I cautiously slipped out of the saddle and tied Koko to a tree. Mr. Stall buckled a halter on the gelding and handed me the lead rope. From that day forward, he called me Marian. Much to my surprise, what began as a hair-raising exchange with a cranky horseman turned out to be an unexpected adventure with a lonely, ill tempered, widower who taught us plenty about how to care for a horse. Soon Robin and I would share his small world of oats, liniment, and horseracing memories from years past. We learned about Dan Patch, a pacer who set a record for covering a quarter mile in one minute fifty-five seconds, as a nine-year-old. The record lasted for thirty-two years. Old Bob also talked

Who Shall We Be?

about the great horse Hambletonian and the Hambletonian Stakes, a famous race that began in 1926, at the New York State Fair.

Once we became acquainted, Bob taught us how to care for our horses' hooves, and how to give them a proper bath. He also agreed to shoe Koko. One day he drove us to the Chippewa County Fairground harness racing stable to meet his old friend, George Ashe. The two of them talked about trading horses in Fort Dodge, Iowa, and winning races in Milwaukee. Robin and I sat on a tack trunk, listening to tales about runaways on the racetrack, overturned sulkies, and screaming fans. When we got home, I tried to explain it all to my mom. She looked at me brightly and suggested that we invite Bob to join us for coffee and cake.

At first nobody believed that old Bob Stall let two horse crazy girls come onto his property. The fact that he joined us for coffee and cake must have been quite a mystery to those who knew him. We learned that he had a reputation for running people out of his barn and out of his life. Robin and I didn't know all this, though my mother did. We girls had no understanding of the loneliness that haunted him since his wife died in a car accident years earlier. All we knew was we couldn't get enough of his stories about grandstand calamities and racetrack speed records. As for his own geldings, he said they once had been great prospects at the track. That was until one suffered from a life-threatening puncture wound to his chest by running into a metal fence post. The other horse shin-bucked during his early training, causing an injury of the cannon bone that ended his racing career. The puncture wound required months of care and ultimately left a jagged scar. In both cases, the geldings required more rehabilitation than their trainers chose to invest. That was when Bob agreed to take them home and nurse them back to health. I never learned whether he later raced either horse again, or did he simply enjoy their company.

Robin and I had stumbled into the world of an isolated old fellow. Life's losses had shut him down. His horses comprised his circle of friends. Old newspaper clippings provided his only social contact. And now our unusual friendship had lured Bob into my mother's kitchen for coffee and cake.

His visit to our home resulted in a level of hospitality and warmth that he likely had never known. Though Mom's horse experience was limited, she wasted no time getting to questions that inspired Bob to light up. "How did you come to love harness racehorses? What was your most exciting race? How old were you when you raced your first horse? Do you have a favorite horse? What makes him a favorite?"

Robin and I watched silently. It was if my mother had turned a light on his path. She simply offered her genuine hospitality to this solitary old guy who finally said yes, to letting another adult into his life. Robin and I might not have called Bob's problem loneliness. Yet, we could see that our mutual love of horses, plus Mom's good food and respectful questions served as an invitation to rejoin the world around him.

Witnessing this amazing change in old Bob, I was reminded of a time my mother gave me the entire collection of A.A. Milne's Winnie-the-Pooh. We both loved the books and often wrote down quotes from the characters and taped them to the refrigerator. One quote came to mind, as I absorbed the meaning of our friendship with Bob Stall. *"Piglet noticed that even though he had a very small heart, it could hold a rather large amount of gratitude."*

Piglet's short statement spoke volumes about how my mother conducted her life. For me, her deep faith and genuine interest in family and beyond bore much evidence of holiness—holiness, as in the Scottish word hale, highlights health, happiness, and wholeness. Beyond her companionable nature, she grasped the meaning of good living. She lived this through her music, her friendships, her kindness, and even in the comical ways that inspired her discipline of us children.

Years earlier, during the Great Depression when her family had very little money, she learned that to celebrate life together meant to appreciate its mix of hues and moods. She knew what it meant to be present to the daily experience of possibilities. She also genuinely enjoyed the beauty of creation and the fundamental goodness of life. Considering her rocky beginning, my mother grew into life of genuine kindness and inclusiveness of those who live alone or have been separated from life's joys.

The challenging thing about loneliness is it can be prevented through good personal relationships. In most cases, averting loneliness doesn't even require medicine, professional care, or a big budget. We can reach out like Mom dared to do. We can visit. We can include others by inviting them to join our activities and get togethers. We can initiate deeper, more meaningful conversations that help others feel seen and loved.

Our country's recent history of pandemics, social, intellectual, and political polarization have created an environment that invites human separation and loneliness. Though this epidemic is not going to simply go away, we can impact it by shifting our focus on healing and preventing the spread of isolation and loneliness. We can make it happen, just as my mother made it happen with an ornery old horseman. It was nothing fancy, but she, and of course, Robin and I, demonstrated the power of reaching out with kindness until we literally wore old Bob down. Hopefully he finally realized that we were crazy about him and truly wanted to make his life better. I do know that he also made our lives better.

An Informed Response to Immigration

"I come from a family of immigrants," explained a young Mexican man who works in Wisconsin's dairy industry. Most of my friends do as well. Though our ancestors were generally welcomed in the United States, they also worked hard and set high expectations for themselves and their families. Conversely,

Who Shall We Be?

today Mexicans who come to the United States seeking agricultural employment face more than the prospect of border walls and harsh judgment. They also are likely to find themselves leaving behind their loved ones and their culture.

So, why would American farmers seemingly make their lives more complicated by hiring immigrant workers? More than 20 years ago, a fifth generation Wisconsin dairy farmer named John Rosenow found himself with no choice in the matter. He tried to recruit for jobs that now pay between $32,000 and $42,000 a year, plus on-farm housing, if needed. But the unrelenting routine of milking, birthing, feeding and cleaning is one Rosenow says Americans long ago stopped wanting to do. For years, he has tried to recruit Americans through local farm supply stores and beyond, though has not had a single response. Nobody even applied for the jobs. Desperate for laborers, he eventually hired a Mexican immigrant he found through a farm magazine advertisement.

"Manuel came and milked fifty-four days straight," explained John. "Here was somebody who worked as hard as I do. After his 54 days, Manuel returned home. "Wow, this looked like an answer to my biggest problem, labor." Today, John employs fifteen Mexicans. Including Roberto Tecpile. Not only does Roberto feed, clean and manage cattle, he is skilled at repairing farm equipment, a real asset on a big dairy farm

Today, Wisconsin's dairy industry reports that most of its workers are immigrants, an arrangement that endures despite the rancorous debate about immigration. "My wife and I are dairy farmers who now employ a team of Mexican immigrants," said John. "They come from an area called Zongolica, in the State of Veracruz. Our employees live on the farm in the housing we provide. We have been employers for over fifty years, and of Mexicans for the last 26 years."

John also places a high value on good management. "From the very start of my career, I have wanted to be the best boss each of my employees would ever have," he emphasized. "I also feel that we owe them more than a paycheck. We must offer the best leadership within the constraints of a viable industry. Additionally, for me to be a good employer, I must know the wants and needs of my employees so that I can provide them with a fulfilling life. This is a difficult task, made even more difficult when the employee comes from a different culture and speaks a different language. This also explains, why I quickly accepted the opportunity to travel to Mexico and visit the families of my employees. I realized this would contribute immeasurably to my understanding of my team. It proved to be even more important than I ever imagined."

Who Shall We Be?

The first trip, in 2001, lasted ten days, a week of intensive language classes followed by time for the farmers to meet their workers' families.

A journalist traveled with the group that first year. After the farmers had completed visits with their employees' families, they boarded a bus. The bus headed down the road, until

a local journalist traveling with the group asked the driver to stop. Everyone got out of the bus, and the journalist proceeded to tell them that they were the first employers to come this far to see the families left behind. By all accounts, this was unheard of in Mexico. "As I thought about the journalist's remarks, I felt they were absurd," John" exclaimed. "How else would one become a great boss without making such an effort? Why were we the first?"

Upon returning home from that trip, John learned that word about their visit had spread among his employees. "Fortunately, I had a photo of our travel group and the families who had come to see us in the main Zocolo in Orizaba. I made copies of that photo and gave them to each of our employees." "Later those photos showed up on the walls of their apartments."

John has now taken the trip ten times. Each time he finds himself overwhelmed by the progress these families have made. "Thanks to our employees who share their earnings, their families have moved out of poverty to a place within middle class" he described. "New homes are being built, children are being educated, and daily lives include much more than survival. Clearly my employees are making a difference for their families."

"It became clear that our visits to Mexico to meet these families was a real value. For example, on a later trip, we and our interpreter, Shaun Duvall, were enjoying the hospitality of coffee and traditional dishes with a current employees' family. A small boy kept running in and out of the house, hiding behind his mother at times. We eventually were introduced to him. His name was John. They had named their sone after me! How could one ask for a higher honor than that? "Young John is now reported to be working in New York State," said John Senior. "I wonder if I will ever meet him again."

Meanwhile, Gustavo came to our farm from Tlacipa in 2021. He has learned English in the class we offer each Monday afternoon. In 2023 we stopped in Tlacipa to visit others, as we always do. Gustavo's mother, son and daughter came to visit us from their home out in the rural area. She told us the story of her husband who had died from stomach cancer in the last six months. Gustavo had pondered returning to Mexico when that happened, but he knew the family needed money to live, so he stayed on our farm and sent money home. As she told the story, her eyes and ours filled with tears.

Who Shall We Be?

"One of the things I hear so often from some of our political leaders is, "They are not sending us their best," said John. "I've now been to those villages where our guys come from and can see that they sent us their best. They sent us the leaders of their communities. They sent us a lawyer. They sent us a medical student. They have a great work ethic, they are honest, and they are the kind of people one would like to have as neighbors. Gustavo calls every week to see if the family is okay. The money he sends home allows his brother and sister to stay in school. His mother replied, we have no needs that are not met because Gustavo takes care of us. At age of 21, Gustavo has taken on the role of breadwinner in the family. Because he has selflessly dedicated himself to that role, their lives are so much better.

The background story of these visits began in1999. It has increased in popularity among farmers and has become an annual event. Carl Duley, Buffalo County Wisconsin UW-Extension agricultural agent, had already identified a need to bridge the communication gap between local farmers and their Mexican employees. He initially approached Shaun Duvall, the local high school Spanish teacher about this need. Carl asked Shaun to start offering language classes for the immigrants.

Shaun's responded with a concern that the migrants would not learn enough Spanish in a twenty-hour class. She did, however, believe they needed something more. So, she began teaching Spanish and providing interpreting services for a group of local farmers.

Soon it became clear that language combined with cultural issues would benefit from additional support services. This combination of challenges prompted Shaun to plan and subsequently lead that first trip to Mexico with a group of fifteen farmers. During the trip, they immersed themselves in Spanish language classes, cultural immersion experiences, and visits with employees' families. John Rosenow participated in that first cultural exchange visit. He described the experience as life-changing for him. Upon returning home, he wanted to do whatever he could to make the Mexican trips happen again. This was when he and Shaun Duvall began planning a powerful resource, a nonprofit that helps ease this multifaceted immigration task. Puentes/Bridges specializes in creating practical services that enable immigrant employees to successfully transition within their new homes. They offer a comprehensive resource guide that includes information about health care, worker's rights, driving, managing legal matters, immigrations system, food shelf, pantries, and much more. This rich source of support services helps farmers, and their Mexican crews build community with one another. Additionally, the Mexican trips continue to connect farmers to their employees' families by delivering yet another opportunity to help support relationships.

"Ours is a politically conservative area," explained Shaun. "Yet suddenly we had experienced an influx of people who did not share our culture or language. They needed help. The development of Puentes/Bridges emphasizes people and their desire to deepen their connections with one another. Their focus lies in fostering this desire and strengthening relationships."

That first trip, in 2001, eventually referred to as "Cultural Immersion—A Puentes Experience," lasted ten days. When the group showed up there were four different local Mexican television stations present to film the event. Several families showed up as well. "They were dressed in their best and were so honored that the employers of their brothers, sons or cousins would come all the way from the United States to get to know them as human beings," said current Puentes director, Mercedes Falk. A week of intensive language classes began, followed by farmers meeting the workers' families. Those meetings quickly took center stage. As their guide, Shaun also realized how important these personal interactions were. The experience was so illuminating and life changing for the farmers that, in 2003, Shaun and John Rosenow, who also joined that original trip, created Puentes/Bridges. Since then, over 150 farmers and various community members have travelled to Mexico to immerse themselves in the culture of their employees.

The trips began with a wish to learn the language, yet they also produced opportunities to make other family connections. When dairy producers meet wives, parents, children, sisters, and brothers of their employees, a bond is created that often results in employee longevity and productivity. Most important, it builds strong connections between people of very different cultures, but with similar wants and needs. "All it requires is a desire to learn and understand another person's world," said John. You don't even need all the right words to achieve this."

Since that first trip, dairy producers and community members have been traveling to Mexico, principally to rural Veracruz and surrounding states like Oaxaca, Hidalgo, and Puebla. The goal is always to visit families and better understand the culture of the employees that come to work on farms in Southeastern Minnesota and West Central Wisconsin. When dairy producers meet wives, parents, children, sisters, and brothers of their employees, a bond is created that often results in employee longevity and productivity. Most importantly, it helps build strong connections between people of very different cultures, yet with similar wants and needs.

"When the relatives in Mexico say to the farmer, 'I entrust my sons to you,' that is a big moment," Shaun added.

Who Shall We Be?

Puentes/Bridges has become famous for taking an issue, surrounding immigration, and making it a human story rather than a political problem devoid of humanity. Puentes has attracted worldwide attention. Shaun Duval has been awarded the highest accolade given by the Mexican government to a non-citizen. It has been featured in stories and documentaries in Holland, Japan, Denmark, and other parts of the world. Most large publications have covered Puentes, because it's an organization that adds a rich layer of humanity to immigration. They achieve this by using stories of real people doing wonderful things while just living their lives. Realistically that will never go out of fashion no matter where the political winds take us.

A new generation of Puentes outreach began when Mercedes Falk took over the organization's leadership. The website offers links to past articles. News stories invariably result in people from all over wanting to help with money or ideas. Mercedes has attracted immigrants to serve on the board of directors. No doubt the scope of what Puentes does will increase, though the original goal of bringing cultures together to engage in a great experience rather than a poor one will continue.

Seven to ten farmers accompany Mercedes to Mexico on each year's trip. Often, they travel to the state of Veracruz, which many Wisconsin dairy workers call home. The farmers pay their own way, approximately $2,000, for a weeklong trip.

The creation of Puentes/Bridges has also introduced a host of new services designed to support immigrant farm workers during their time in America. For example, they have developed a resource guide that includes information on everything from health care and workers' rights, to driving, handling legal matters, immigration system function, foods shelves, pantries, and more. The goal is simply to help American farmers, and their immigrant employees build mutual trust and satisfaction with their employment. This success comes with shared language, cultural understanding, and acceptance which translates to helping farming communities

"Ours is a politically conservative area," explained Shaun. "Yet suddenly we experienced an influx of people who didn't share our culture or language. They needed help, and we have found ways to offer it."

The development of Puentes/Bridges, emphasizes people and their desire to deepen their connections with one another. The focus lies in fostering this desire and strengthening relationships.

Today the program's overarching goal is relationship building. John Rosenow, who has previously served on the Puentes/Bridges board of directors, says the program has

Who Shall We Be?

helped him gain insight into the lives of his employees who risk detention, or even worse, in their quest for a better life.

"I now better understand their motivation to put themselves in danger, to come here and to work in a different culture, and to make money, largely to support their families" he said.

The effort runs counter to the anti-Immigrant sentiment fueled by many political leaders today. Unfortunately, negative rhetoric and aggressive policies have included family separation at the border and a sharp uptick in arrests by U.S. Immigration and Customs Enforcement.

Finally, people tend to ask for economic data when discussing immigration. What does a cultural situation like this do for me? Simply Improving humanity is not always enough. Improving our economic outlook while achieving human relationships tends to be more palatable. Consider the fact that there are currently 23 million undocumented immigrants in the US. The data says that more businesses have been started by immigrants on a per capita basis than native born individuals. Additionally, crime statistics show that immigrants are involved in fewer crimes than native born individuals. Add to this, in the dairy industry, immigrants dominate. There are estimates that almost 90 percent of the milk produced by cows in our country is harvested by immigrants. Meat packing is very similar. It is safe to say that at every meal our food has been touched by immigrant hands. Nothing is quite as personal as the food we put into our bodies every day.

This leads one to wonder: Do we really know a good neighbor when we meet one?

Are We Awake Yet?

Recently I spoke at length with a Catholic priest friend, the Reverend John Heagle. Our conversation focused on a troubling and complex topic, our world's various crises that have felt and sometimes still feel beyond our personal and our countries' comprehension and control. Unsurprisingly the conversation began with COVID-19, a devastating pandemic and major health crisis that reached across the globe. Today it remains a troubling long-term problem for many individuals. Our conversation then moved beyond this shattering health crisis to other calamities that have been unfolding for years. In many ways we have become so numb to these other slow-motion catastrophes that they have morphed into a form of white noise, "the sound of silence," John added. For example, beyond the catastrophic results of a pandemic, we have been able to compartmentalize important issues such as: global warming, systemic racism, unjust economic systems, unending wars, nuclear weapons, broken criminal justice systems, worldwide suffering of the poor, and vicious political and cultural polarization.

Rather than offer a list of heroic measures for resolving these problems, John wondered out loud about a deeper crisis that has been unfolding for decades. As a priest who has spent a lifetime immersed in peace and justice ministries at home and abroad, he lamented about the persistent silence surrounding some of our worlds' most urgent and pending crises.

"Why have we been so stymied by these multi-layered catastrophes?" John sighed. "From the rainforests of Brazil to the murder of unarmed black men in our streets, from the vicious polarization of our political and cultural discourse to the dying songbirds and the Mexican families facing separation and deportation from our country. "Mother Earth and her oppressed children must be crying out in lament" he concluded.

The title of Dr. Martin Luther King's last book asked a question: *Where do we go from here, Chaos or Community?* "In the fifty-two years since he wrote those words, there has clearly been more chaos than community," John concluded. "The persistence of structural violence has shattered any dream of genuine kinship. Now we are, yet again, hearing a wake-up call for our wounded world. The question is whether we will finally respond to this urgent summons. In our moments of clarity, many of us recognize that we can no longer return to business as usual, nor can we engage in the illusion of going back to normal life. How will we respond when we finally comprehend that what we call 'normal is, realistically, a destructive pattern that threatens the future of life on our planet? Willing or not, we are confronting a major turning point in human history," he concluded. "What will it take to wake us up? What does it mean for us to choose life? Where is the path toward hope?"

Reasons for Hope

Tentative signs of awakening offer some genuine hope. For example, early and enduring initiatives on behalf of the earth and its future have provided a foundation of-encouragement. For more than a century the environmental movement has been a strong, if an alternative force for change. From John Muir, Aldo Leopold, and Rachel Carson to, Maneka Gandhi, Wendell Berry, Erin Brockovitch, Al Gore, and Bill McKibben, prophetic voices that have raised our civic awareness. Even my mother made every effort to show her friends and family the beauty and fragility of our earth. And she never stopped telling us why we must help protect it. "Scientists, eco-theologians, oceanographers, and the

Green Movement, continue to gather data to convince and educate an often-skeptical public of global warming," said john. Earth Day has been celebrated for forty years. More recently, inspiration has been provided by the visionary voice of Greta Thunberg. Perhaps, the most important development finds that young people have taken up the environmental cause with renewed passion.

"From the perspective of global religious leadership, Pope Francis has clearly articulated the urgency of caring for our 'common home," added John. "His encyclical *Laudato si,* addresses the growing crisis of the environment. He also focuses on the relationship between the devastation of the natural world and the suffering of the poor. His vision offers a striking example of integrating environmental concerns with eco-justice." The environmental movement focuses primarily on humanity's negative impact on the ecosphere. Eco-justice builds on the same mission, though also addresses the interconnection between environmental destruction and its adverse impact on oppressed people. "Simply stated, justice reveals that poor populations suffer far more from environmental destruction than richer citizens," added John. "Pope Francis reminds us that '*a true ecological approach always becomes a social approach. It must integrate questions of justice in debates on the environment, so that one hears both the cry of the earth and the cry of the poor."*

For those of us who live a relatively comfortable life in purported advanced nations, the demands of eco-justice are not typically within in our awareness, let alone our commitment. Nevertheless, the leaders of the environmental movement, the insistent voices of the young, and the emergence of eco-justice offer reasons for hope. "Yet, hope is not the same as optimism," added John. "The road to hope is rocky, risky, and unending. It does not depend on rhetoric or even realism. It does not count on the good will of people or the ten-year plan of any institution. Hope is a commitment to keep on acting on behalf of justice without counting the personal cost or measuring the outcomes. It is, in short, a call to radical trust that expresses itself in concrete action."

John and I agree that it is so difficult to predict what it will take to mobilize the human community for this kind of change. Surely it will require more than speech-making, more than an election, more than winning culture wars, and particularly more than applying Band-Aids to our current economic, social, and religious institutions. We further agreed, that, at its core, this is a *spiritual* crisis. In an interview during the nation-wide protests following the murder of George Floyd in Minneapolis, Harvard University philosophy professor Cornell West said, "Our culture is so market-driven—everything for sale, everybody for sale—it can't deliver the kind of nourishment for soul, for meaning, or for purpose," Clearly, the ache in our hearts is also a cry for "nourishment of soul, for meaning, and for purpose." We need science, political acumen, and international collaboration, but this will not be enough. The call goes deeper. It is a call to communal conversion, a mandate for a radical transformation of human consciousness.

"So, how do we move toward this challenging truth?" I asked John. "Clearly the first step is to break through our corporate" denial," he noted. "Yet, even if we succeed at this, history suggests that we must further acknowledge the power of white privilege. It's likely that I share this reality with most of my fellow white citizens in the developed world," he added.

Psychologists tell us that denial is an understandable and even necessary trait. T.S. Eliot reminds us that humankind cannot bear very much reality. We all engage in some forms of denial just to make our way through the daily labyrinth of life. "But denial becomes destructive when it prevents us from facing the lived truth of our lives," John added. "Perhaps the most painful recent example of this form of denial was the initial failure of our government, and many of its citizens to act decisively when confronted by the devastating impact of COID-19."

"Awakening from 'normal' consciousness is a major theme in all world religions. However, we cannot wake up from this 'civilized slumber' if we do not first recognize that we have been in some essential way, asleep at the wheel," John concluded. "Realistically, most of us in more affluent nations have been, in effect, sleepwalking for decades. Even as it moves inexorably toward midnight, we have kept our finger firmly on the snooze button of the doomsday clock. The clock is still ticking, and we are still snoozing." Additionally, this protracted state of unawareness has revealed that we have, without recognizing it, become dependent on various forms of societal addiction. These include everything from consumerism and the free market to unfettered capitalism, to the nuclear arms race, and to redemptive violence, economic inequality, environmental devastation, and the illusion of unrestrained technological progress.

"We are at the beginning of a mass extinction," Greta Thunberg once told the UN General Assembly, and all you can talk about is money.

"The truth will make you free," Jesus tells us, and we might add, but first it will make you miserable.

Are we flirting with An Apocalyptic Crisis?

To state the obvious, we are facing a crisis that parallels or exceeds any in our history. This is an apocalyptic moment. "I am not referring to the usual doomsday scenario as preached by many fundamentalist Christians," John adds. "This apocalypse does not refer to some divine intervention to destroy the world in a cataclysm of violence. It is, on the contrary, a catastrophe that we ourselves have created and for which we must take full responsibility."

The Greek word for apocalypse means to uncover, to disclose, or to reveal. COVID-19 pulled back the curtain of denial and revealed the landscape of systemic injustice. "It is uncovering the long, unfolding, self-inflicted devastation that we are wreaking on our environment. This, plus the build-up of nuclear weapons, as well as the global inequality between those who have resources for food, health care, and safe living conditions, and those who do not," added John.

The protracted health problems and death toll from COVID-19 continue to remind us that this virus plus any new viruses such as Bird Flu invariably target those who have an underlying condition. It also has unveiled another fundamental truth, that all of us share a single underlying condition. It's called the human condition, the most vital of all gifts and the most urgent of all predicaments. It carries with it the ultimate challenge of taking responsibility, of embracing our shared freedom to choose a new path for the future.

Can we Re-imagining the Role of Religion?

"Most spiritual traditions, including my own, are facing a critical turning point," John pointed out "Either we reclaim our founding vision and re-imagine it for the future, or my nieces and nephews, their children, and most spiritual seekers will find our teaching to be increasingly irrelevant. For example, a young college woman born and raised in a devout Catholic family, recently told me that, in her experience, the Church is continuing to give the same worn-out answers to questions that we are no longer asking. For example, the New 'Creation Story' is shaping the hopes and actions of many scientists, cosmologists, and spiritual seekers, but has not yet found a viable place in our preaching or Catechesis."

At the same time, we are seeing encouraging signs of renewal," continued John. "In my religious tradition, despite times of regression, the seeds sown by the Vatican are still finding good soil. In addition to *Laudato si* and its call to care for the earth, Pope Francis continues to advocate for restorative justice in the human community. After centuries of theological and ecclesiastical justification, he recently called for the abolition of the death penalty. Along with this advance in moral conviction, there is a parallel development in the church's teaching and practice of Gospel non-violence. Many Christians are not aware of this emerging vision that challenges us to embrace biblical justice and peacemaking as a way of life, an effective method of resolving domestic, national and international conflicts. In large part this is due to the courageous witness of nonviolent peacemakers in the most troubled parts of our world. These encouraging steps are hopeful signs for the Catholic community and its leaders who often cling to the illusion that the church is the last mountain to move. The challenge now is that we no longer have the leisure of taking our time. If this is an apocalyptic crisis, it must also become an authentic Catholic moment."

Can We Grow Up in Time?

'Timothy Ferris published a book titled Coming of Age in the Milky Way, in 1998. "His goal was to invite readers to explore the scientific discoveries of the twentieth century and their positive implications for our time," John explained. "When I finished the book, I recall the wave of optimism that washed over me. Now, thirty-two years later, I am aware that I was mistaking intellectual enthusiasm for realistic hope. Given our wounded world, picturing ourselves as 'coming of age' in our galaxy is, at best, breezy optimism, and at worst, simply arrogance."

Who Shall We Be?

Considering the evidence, we have a lot of growing up to do. Spiritually, scientifically, politically, culturally, and globally, we have a lot of growing up to do. It might be more correct to say that we are still trying to work our way through early adolescence – the middle school of maturity. At this point, our human community appears to be fixated on rituals of narcissism, short sightedness, and instant gratification. Little wonder that many scientists doubt if we will be around long enough to come of age as a human species.

Nonetheless, research scientists found a vaccine for COVID-19. It remains to be seen whether deeper challenges such as the awakening of our moral imagination will also bloom. If so, will it lead to the transformation of consciousness necessary to shape our future? I believe it will. Hope has feet. And we are still walking.

Retire or transition? This is the question

Recently Mary, a friend and work colleague has been sharing her thoughts about creating a new business. We have worked together for years, as she has made her way through the development of several successful enterprises. It was her most recent success within the field of health care leadership that prompted Mary's interest in trying something new.

I've always valued Mary's energy and timely inspirations, and this one certainly captured my attention. During recent years

Who Shall We Be?

she, has applied her leadership and coaching skills in ways that have helped rebalance health care organization's leaders, board members, and teams of employees. Daunting setbacks created by the Covid-19 pandemic prompted a host of organizational and financial challenges for healthcare organizations. Additionally, she discovered that many of these leaders who had successfully guided their organizations through a uniquely stressful experience, were now beginning to discuss the alure of retirement.

As Mary and I continue to share our thoughts about what this new endeavor might look like, I suggested that the word retirement coaching might not appeal to everyone. Perhaps she could expand her audience by including individuals who wish to transition from a demanding career to a more inviting one that can be sustained as one ages. In fact, transitioning from years of hospital chaplaincy to writing and teaching has been a rewarding path for me. I have discovered that, like retirement, successful transitioning also benefits from careful thought and planning. It creates a rich opportunity for identifying one's personal values and goals. Serious self-examination typically reveals valuable ideas plans, and spiritual journeys that might have been neglected during one's career. I also have enjoyed discovering that aging and creative expression do not need to retire early. They simply need to be nurtured and guided.

The truth is, as we age, we also begin to understand the value of our history, our friendships, family, achieved goals, missed goals, opportunities, healing, spiritual growth, and much more. Simply walking out the door of our career or life work and thinking that all will go swimmingly, is naive, at best, and wasteful at worst. The enlightening conversations I've enjoyed with Mary have invited me to look more carefully at my own development and value system. It has provided an opportunity for me to recognize how much I have enjoyed by transitioning instead of retiring. This does not mean that I have simply given up life as a hospital chaplain, or a health care communications professional. What it does mean is I have begun writing and teaching others what I have learned about the importance of healing, wholeness, and happiness.

In fact, I have been fortunate to have grown up in a family of transitioning specialists. Most of my relatives, including my grandfather, father, uncle and brother have worked in the law business. Hence, as my brother aged and became tired of practicing criminal law, he chose to transition into probate law. Even my father, a circuit court judge for most of his adult life, never fully retired. Instead, he turned to writing jury instruction for the University of Wisconsin law school. It was a perfect transition for a man who also loved to spend time fly fishing and duck hunting with his favorite dog Rufus.

Who Shall We Be?

Sometimes Transitions require a Gentle Hand

Aging has offered me many opportunities to learn, grow, travel, and explore. It also has shown me that I'm reluctant to let go of everything, from my mother's collection of cookbooks and favorite holiday foods to my childhood bed, Christmas dishes, Christmas tree ornaments, and Grandma Cook's 's large portrait that hangs above my dining room table. My move from Wisconsin to Minnesota nearly crippled the movers for all the heavy antique bookcases, fireplace screens, and old fashion cookware that might not ever see the heat of a stove. It was difficult to let go of what felt like the family in which I grew up. However, once I made the move and began sorting out my feelings about "letting go" of my history, I began to understand what one might call a different, yet significant kind of transition.

This was when I received a call from an older family friend named Louise. She surprised me when she announced her decision to sell her lovely home and move into a nearby senior living center. Having experience my parents downsizing and selling their home of 40, years, I knew this was no easy task. Not only did it involve saying goodbye to many chapters of their lives, it included the task of physically separating and disposing of everything from furniture and photos to wine glasses, canning jars, countless photos, antiques, family history and much more.

What would they take with them, and what would they leave behind? What would they give away, and what might they sell? From family history to favorite coffee cups, it became a great debate. And that was before anybody had given much thought to the actual move.

I quickly learned that this part also involved more than saying goodbye. It required additional hours of sorting, cleaning, packing, measuring, lugging furniture and explaining to the movers that antiques required special attention. Then came the move into a new apartment. Not only was it much smaller than my parent's home, but the process again required sorting, cleaning, unpacking, measuring and more. It would not be an exaggeration to say that this moving business demands a calm temperament, a sense of humor, and first-rate arm strength.

I must admit the whole event prepared me for later moves. It also reminded me of an innovative, local moving business located in our area. They offered a clear and much simpler approach to this arduous task. That was when I suggested to Louise that we contact Gentle Transitions. I knew they specialize in senior relocations and enjoyed a reputation as national leaders in the senior moving industry.

It seemed like an opportunity that Louise might appreciate. After sharing my family experience with her, I suggested that she try Gentle Transitions. I also offered to

Who Shall We Be?

participate in the planning and preparation for the move. It felt like a valuable experience for each of us, as I already knew that senior relocations tend to invite anxiety and frustrations for everyone.

Gentle Transitions of Edina, Minnesota has become a local and national leader in the senior moving industry. Founded in 1990 by Mercedes and Bernie Gunderson of Edina, it also boasts a plethora of clients from all over the United States. The company's unique services begin immediately when they are hired. At that point, the client is assigned what is called a *move manager*. This individual then proceeds to lead the way throughout the cleaning, sorting, packing, and unpacking. They gently tackle everything that tends to create anxiety and exhaustion.

In September of 2024, a similar moving organization called WellRive purchased and then integrated several more move management organizations across the nation under the WellRive name. Each of these companies maintains strong reputations for delivering high-quality, compassionate services.

As someone who has experienced these challenges, I agree that it takes the right kind of person to do this work with grace and dignity. The day I met Louis's move manager I understood what a value she brought to the table.

For example, move managers work with floor plans of each client's new space to help them figure which of their belongings will and will not fit. I took part in each of these steps and understood that the most glaring stumbling block when making a transition is that the client has accumulated so much, and they don't know where to begin. People often need their hand held during this process. I appreciated that the move manager led my friend through her home, measuring furniture, sorting art and photos, and exploring the kitchen cupboards and dishwasher. This enabled her to select everything from cleaning products to cookware and an entertainment center that would fit the new space.

Most Gentle Transitions clients leave their homes and move into independent living, condominiums, senior co-ops, or assisted/memory care environments. There is no average age. Gentle Transitions has moved clients as young as twenty-six and is happy to help clients at any stage of life. It was a good choice.

Experiencing the moving process with my aging parents and my friend Louise prompted me to think about the paths we take as we age. Why are we making a transition, and how can we contribute to the quality of this change rather than simply resist it? Author and teacher Parker Palmer offers a powerful thought in his book *Let Your Life Speak*. "Before you tell your life what you intend to do with it, listen for what it intends to do with you. Before you tell your life what truths and values you have decided to live up to, let your life tell you what truths you embody and what values you represent and wish to protect."

Doctor Palmer's words invite us to grow into our authentic selves at any age. This does not mean simply growing old. He asks us to discern, to take a self-inventory, and reflect. How do we wish to participate in the world around us?

Where do we find our joy? How do we wish to engage with our family, friends, neighbors, and strangers? Do we wish to engage in a faith tradition or other spiritual guidance? How do we negotiate hurts and misunderstandings with others? What do we hope for in terms of change? What do we believe about our wounded world? How do we propose to contribute a healing presence to this world?

These steps also help us define our path during times of any life transition. Whether a transition involves illness, retirement, leaving our homes, or separation from friends and family members, we benefit from thoughtful planning. For example, when we think about the degree of joy we experience or don't experience, we also need to think about the source of our beliefs, feelings and attitudes.

Additionally, it is essential for us to identify or review our individual gifts or assets that enable us to contribute to the quality of our life and the lives of those we interact with. Am I compassionate, resilient, faithful, hopeful, creative, adaptable, self-accepting, resourceful, forgiving, and welcoming. Finally, how do I respond to life events based on these beliefs, or how might I explore different choices.

Hope, according to University of Minnesota researcher Janice Post-White, constitutes a key spiritual element of healing. Hope provides purpose, direction and a reason for being, no matter our age or life experience. I would add that hope encompasses the assured sense that we can transcend the present situation. It is a fundamental attitude toward life and faith.

Additionally, hope is not an occasional feeling we turn to when we need it. It is a disposition that says the future is an open one, and I can dare to believe it holds integrity. That future good can occur even in the face of loss, an unplanned change of direction, or a wounded world. Hope engages our capacity to see ourselves in a larger landscape a landscape in which we can transcend the present situation whatever that might be.

I would further describe hope as a light that shows us our way along the path. In my experience and that of patients and friends, this light can be informative. It can provide a new or undiscovered awareness of a difficult life event or a loss. In some cases, this light on the path has also offered insight into my own opinions and behavior. On other occasions, it has given me the strength to live my convictions.

Who Shall We Be?

Finally, I believe that who we are and what impact we have on our world depends largely on personal courage. Do we have the courage to touch human suffering, our own or others? There is certainly no shortage of it. This is the place where, in the words of Carl Jung, "invited, even not invited, God is present." These are powerful, and sometimes simple situations in which we can present a hopeful presence to those who might feel exhausted, discouraged, invisible, and without hope. And, in the end, isn't it hope that we wish to bring to light?

We live in a culture that reminds us that we are what we do. We are important if we do something important. We are intelligent if we do something clever or valuable. In short, individual achievements and acquisitions remain synonymous with success and joy. However, ultimately the rewards we gain come, not Juist from our high points or outstanding accomplishments. They also immerge from our setbacks, struggles, and our willingness to be transformed and grow. These are the stories and events that shape us. Discovering how we heal from life's challenges and transitions includes discovering important truths about ourselves, our beliefs, and our relationships with the world around us.

Given this big menu, readers might think that I'm naïve when I say we are being called to be a beloved community. In fact, I'm talking about more than our life transitions or the future of our neighborhoods and churches. I'm talking about a practical, unpolished love that respects and seeks good for others as well as for ourselves. This would be the Nelson Mandela, Archbishop Desmond Tutu kind of love. Let's get started.

Today I Will Choose Joy—A discussion guide

Growing toward Happiness

The term heartfelt happiness explored in the following ten steps highlights a way of living rather than a way of wining. It invites you to step into a *life review,* an inner process of moving toward worthy goals and contentment. This kind of success inspires wholehearted living. It raises our awareness of what matters most and least; what is most precious, and what we can release.

Success, understood in this context leads to an expansion of personal qualities and assets that rarely appear on a resume. Nor do these abilities such as creativity, compassion, gratitude, and worthiness show up in many job descriptions. Yet each of these and many more comprise a foundation on which we craft our next steps toward successful living.

Whether we have experienced a loss, entered a life transition, or simply believe it's time to take stock and make course adjustments, consider the following guide. Even better, invite friends and family members to join you in a meaningful conversation about things that truly matter.

1, Describe what success means to you.

Many experiences, traditions, and beliefs contribute to our idea of success. We're a culture that likes to measure everything, from job performance and unemployment numbers to TV ratings, cholesterol, stress levels, and Facebook friends. While traditional measurements of success provide value on some levels, other quality measures contribute to our wellbeing.

Ask yourself

What three things bring me the most, though perhaps simplest joy?

What, outside of work and personal responsibilities, engenders feelings of accomplishment?

When do I feel as if I'm contributing the most? The least?

Beyond specific achievements, what nurtures my self-esteem and sense of delight?

On a scale of one to ten, how would I rate my level of success?

What could I add or remove from my life that would enhance my success?

2. Pay Attention to your beliefs

It's so easy to drift through life paying scant attention to our goals, relationships, and surroundings. One day we are twenty-five charging out to join the flow. The next, we see that time has moved forward, though we might not have done the same. Using our beliefs to resist transitions comes easily to most of us, even when that change promises to improve the quality of our lives.

Ask yourself

Name some dreams you held in your twenties, forties, sixties.

Which of these dreams have you realized?

What has it felt like to not fulfill certain dreams?

What dreams and hopes do you hold at this moment?

When has a life change caused you to feel stuck?

Have people or expectations made it hard to move forward?

Do you have the will and the resources to shift direction?

What will life feel like if you choose to remain in the same place?

3. Review Your Assets

Whether interviewing someone for a book, or engaging in the work of a hospital chaplain, I have been amazed at the emotional and spiritual assets people possess. Some of these qualities come naturally. Others develop when someone faces a life challenge. Most people tell me that their best asset has helped them move beyond a challenge. Most also tell me that their best asset has helped them move beyond a serious interruption toward a renewed or rewarding new path. Assets come in all shapes and sizes, from optimism and joyfulness to courage and faith. Begin with the list below and add your own.

Ask yourself

Most of us possess qualities we either don't value or rarely reveal. For example, a serious illness can inspire remarkable courage and calm. Or the loss of a job might prompt a highly successful professional to grow in humility. What asset do you bring to your work, personal relationships, and decision-making? What role have these assets played in mapping your life direction? What role could they play right now?

> Resilience
>
> Creativity and resourcefulness
>
> Adaptability
>
> Self-worth and a capacity to forgive

4. Stop Resisting

I'm convinced that few of us choose to change much. Instead, we seem to resist going with the flow until all else fails. Moving forward with resilience rather than resistance opens many more opportunities and room for happiness. Saying "Yes," is good for friendships, broadens the possibilities for fun, opens doors to learning something new, and almost always sparks up a dull day.

Ask yourself

> Remember a time when, faced with what felt like a loss or failure, you let go and said, "Yes," to walking forward.
>
> Describe the process and the result of adapting to your new reality.
>
> Most of what we learn in life begins with a question or a problem. List some problems you have negotiated successfully. List some you have had to release.

Name a pivotal point when an unexpected change brought you meaningful new insights and discoveries.

Name a personal quality that helped you make an important transition.

5. Judge Less

It's fair to say that most judging of self and others comes from a place of insecurity or fear of being wrong. Yes, we see plenty of problems, offensive people, and defects in our own personalities. The negativity and injustice surrounding us can truly invite judgment. Sometimes compassion seems beyond reach. Yet, judgment creates a gulf of separation that lacks both love and forgiveness.

Ask yourself, When I am judgmental

Do I feel energized?

Do I foster other's trust and confidence?

Do I win friends?

Do I exhale negativity into the space around me?

Do I close my heart and mind to new people and different ideas?

Ask yourself, When I resist judgment

Do I grow in gratitude and empathy?

Do I Promote happiness and creativity?

Do I focus more on life emerging around me?

Do I give less attention to imperfections?

Do I become a conduit of peace?

6. Heal or Reenergize Relationships

Reenergizing relationships can be as simple as wasting time wisely with a friend, or as complicated as releasing resentments from past hurts. And not every relationship can be healed. Sometimes obstacles such as addictions, long-held resentments, and betrayals make it hard to reach a meeting of the minds with another. In these cases, the answer might require letting go and coming to some level of peace on our own.

Ask yourself

How do I feed, protect, and keep my important relationships strong?

Think of a time when you had to let go of injured feelings about past conflicts.

Recall when you had to reach out to an estranged friend or family member.

Describe a time when you needed to make amends.

What happens when healing a relationship is not an option?

Can you let go knowing you have acted sincerely?

7. Seek to Belong

Psychiatrist Robert Waldinger, MD, director of the a years-long Harvard Study of Adult Development, offers two clear messages from his comprehensive investigation that began in

1938. Loneliness kills, and one of five Americans reports being lonely and isolated. Social connections, including friendships, family and a welcoming faith community engender happiness, better health and more meaningful lives. Belonging involves coming together peaceably with others and enables us to grow a common vision of respect. Meaningful personal connections and supportive communities literally breathe life into living.

Ask yourself

What does it mean to belong to a community of inclusion and acceptance?

Describe your sources of community and social connections.

When did you last join or create a new community? (book club, walking group, etc.)

Do you routinely unplug from technology in favor of face-to-face meeting?

Recall when you reached out to someone who appeared to be isolated or alone.

How can a community (including a faith community) advocate for its members?

8. Cultivate Humor

You don't need to be a comedian to enjoy a healthy dose of humor. Not only does a good laugh relieve stress, but it also offers a great communication tool with real healing power.

Laughing out loud at ourselves and our observations of the world around us can take the edge off seemingly impossible situations. It also can diffuse anger, fear and grief. I have often heard hospital patients and their families guffawing over irreverent family stories and common memories.

Ask Yourself

What kind of topics and situations do you find funny?

Do you enjoy reading humor or watching funny movies?

Name favorite humorists or comedians that make you laugh.

What makes them funny?

When was the last time you laughed out loud?

9. Have Fun with Food

Many cultures and religions offer a spiritual perspective on food that we have forgotten over the centuries. Most embrace rituals that use food as a means of connecting to a deeper spiritual significance. This includes Jewish, Buddhist, and Muslim faith traditions., among others. For example, Christians sustain a relationship with Jesus Christ through the bread and wine of Holy Communion. From a social standpoint, food wields a mighty power for the comfort it brings to heart, body, and soul.

Ask yourself

Do you view food as a simple necessity, fuel, nourishment, or hospitality?

Describe your relationship with food growing up and today.

How might food heal heart, body, and soul?

How can food serve as a universal language?

How has food connected you to others during times of celebration or sorrow .

10. Don't Postpone Joy

I have heard many patients and friends describe the plans they had been postponing for the future. Some expected to travel or reconnect with old friends. One looked forward to climbing Mt. Kilimanjaro. Another planned to buy a bike, learn to play the piano, and visit Mt. Rushmore. Then something happened that derailed their plans. A significant life interruption. Though we all can't fly off to Paris or seek our bliss by purchasing a ranch in the Colorado mountains, we can find joy and refreshment in unlikely places.

Consider the following and add your own.

Practice saying yes.

Own a pet.

Feed the birds.

Celebrate large and small, don't wait for marriages or birthdays.

Turn off the electronics.

Who Shall We Be?

Be a contributor.

Be a friend.

Be a blessing.

Be the change you wish to see in the world.

Whatever you do, don't postpone joy.

About the Author:

Mary Farr (she/her/hers)

Rev, Deacon Mary Farr, a longtime pediatric and adult hospital chaplain has devoted years to exploring the worlds of hope healing and humor. Mary has published five books and presented for a variety of audiences including: the Hazelden Betty Ford Foundation; the Chautauqua Institution, CaringBridge, and the Minnesota Network of Hospice and Palliative Care. A graduate of the University of Wisconsin, she completed her divinity studies in the Episcopal Diocese of Eau Claire, Wisconsin where she was ordained to the permanent diaconate in 1983. Additionally, she received a Master of Arts degree in Theology from Saint Catherine University, Saint Paul, Minnesota. Mary is currently engaged in faith development and funeral ministry at Trinity Episcopal Church in Excelsior, Minnesota. She honors all faith traditions and spiritual journeys.

Journal Your Thoughts

www.ingramcontent.com/pod-product-compliance
Lightning Source LLC
Chambersburg PA
CBHW051838090426
42736CB00011B/1868